The Fingerprint of God

D1260696

The Fingerprint of God

Reflections on Love and Its Practice

Will Dickerson

RESOURCE *Publications* · Eugene, Oregon

THE FINGERPRINT OF GOD
Reflections on Love and Its Practice

Resource Publications
An Imprint of Wipf and Stock Publishers
199 W. 8th Ave., Suite 3
Eugene, OR 97401

www.wipfandstock.com

PAPERBACK ISBN: 978-1-6667-0487-7
HARDCOVER ISBN: 978-1-6667-0488-4
EBOOK ISBN: 978-1-6667-0489-1

04/15/22

soli Deo gloria

Love (III)

Love bade me welcome; yet my soul drew back,
*   Guilty of dust and sin.*
But quick-eyed Love, observing me grow slack
*   From my first entrance, in*
Drew nearer to me, sweetly questioning
*   If I lack'd anything.*

"A guest," I answer'd, "worthy to be here":
*   Love said, "You shall be he."*
"I, the unkind, ungrateful? Ah, my dear,
*   I cannot look on Thee."*
Love took my hand and smiling did reply,
*   "Who made the eyes but I?*

"Truth, Lord; but I have marr'd them: let my shame
*   Go where it doth deserve."*
"And know you not," says Love, "Who bore the blame?"
*   "My dear, then I will serve."*
"You must sit down," says Love, "and taste my meat."
*   So I did sit and eat.*

—George Herbert (1593-1632)

Contents

Acknowledgements

THIS BOOK HAD A long gestation period. When my first wife, Diane, was battling cancer, several friends urged me to do some writing. That was in 2015. I always saw myself more as a teacher than a writer. Moreover, at that time of my life I lacked the energy for a project such as this, so I resisted. However, these friends persisted. For that, I am grateful. If I remember correctly, it was Sue Berkeley who suggested that I set my thoughts down in the form of reflections. Thank you for the suggestion!

I am very grateful to Matthew and Deborah Dickerson, Nicholas DiFonzo, Bill Murphy, and Rich Shockey for taking the time to read all, or parts, of this book in its earlier manifestations. I am especially grateful for the feedback and suggestions they proffered. I also want to thank the editors associated with Honest Editing (honestediting.com), who didn't pull any punches in suggesting improvements to the manuscript. The book is better because of all of you.

Most of all, I am thankful to my wonderful wife Julia for her love, long-suffering, and encouragement. I doubt I would have completed this project were it not for her. Julia is known for her determination and perseverance, which were on display as she carefully pored through the different versions of the manuscript. She made many helpful suggestions, and she caught many of my errors. She was patient and encouraging. I love her very much!

Whatever faults and shortcomings the reader may find in this work are mine and mine alone.

Introduction: The Faith
of the Atheist

In 1989, THE IRON Curtain suddenly came crashing down with an abrupt-
ness that left the rest of the world with its mouth agape. Very few people
saw this coming. Yet, in the twinkling of an eye, just like that, the Cold
War was over. Even those countries that had been unwilling members of
the Communist Bloc seemed stunned by how rapidly events developed.
Everyone held their breath and waited to see how the Soviet Union would
respond, and when it did nothing, people pinched themselves to make
sure they weren't dreaming.

The nations of Central and Eastern Europe quickly recovered from
their initial shock, and within a year almost all of them had held free elec-
tions for the first time in over a generation. Meanwhile, other nations—
especially those in western Europe—welcomed these former Communist
nations back into fellowship with open arms and tried to reintegrate them
into their network of political and economic alliances. In 1993, as the
aftershocks of this seismic realignment were still being felt, my family
and I moved to Hungary, where I took up a teaching position in a public
secondary school.

At the end of World War II, the Red Army "liberated" Hungary from
the clutches of the Nazis. Unfortunately, the Red Army then forgot to go
home, and Hungary was soon absorbed into the "Soviet sphere of influence"
against its will. Moscow did not waste any time incorporating Hungary into
its totalitarian Communist empire. Officially, Communism was atheistic.
Adherence—at least superficially—to the dogma of atheism was required
by the state. One had to deny the existence of God in order to be admitted
to university. Espousing the tenets of atheism became a prerequisite for

any kind of career advancement. The stubborn refusal to abandon what the government deemed "the outdated vestiges of a decadent Christianity" meant a downgrade in one's housing assignment, a demotion at work, fewer rationing coupons, and possibly much worse.

The curriculum of the Communist educational system was based on a materialistic ideology that denied the existence of any kind of spiritual reality. There was no God. There was not even an "intelligent designer." There was nothing in this universe but energy and matter.

It was not surprising, therefore, that upon our arrival in Hungary, I encountered many who held this materialistic world view. Most did not hold it dogmatically. There were not as many true atheists in Hungary as the former government would have claimed. Many Hungarians believed there probably was some sort of divine being out there, but their beliefs in this area were rather vague. Hence, they did not have too many qualms about compromising with the powers-that-be in order to gain entrance to university, get a promotion at work, or to win the various economic rewards that were doled out to the party faithful.

When the Communist empire collapsed, many decided to take a new look at old-time religion. One of my colleagues said to me, "We could see that the Communists had lied about just about everything, so I wondered if they had lied about God, as well. I figured I would take a look and see for myself." It was easy to see why there were so few true atheists in Hungary. A materialistic world view is deeply unsatisfying. It leaves too many big questions unanswered. Moreover, atheism requires a lot of faith!

Followers of other religions generally admit their belief systems require a certain degree of faith. Many, of course, believe that their system is based on reason and on a certain amount of evidence; nevertheless, they freely admit that at key points their religion does require an act of faith. Their religion has tenets beyond the scope and purview of science to answer. Most atheists, however, refuse to concede that their religion also requires faith and that it is based on assumptions that science and reason simply can not verify. Nevertheless, their *credo,* just like that of other worldviews, is one that must be accepted on faith. Most often, theirs is a faith they come to out of necessity once they have made the *a priori* assumption that there is nothing in the universe but energy and matter. If there is no God, then certain things simply must have happened by themselves.

Over the years, Hungary has produced many world-renown scientists and mathematicians. Hungary is proud of this, and the Hungarian educational system gives a special place to those who excel in mathematics and the natural sciences. Therefore, discussions about the big questions in life often revolve around to what degree science can help us answer some of these big questions.

Science, however, can not tell us *how* or *why* the universe began. It can tell us approximately when it began, and it can tell us how the universe has taken shape since that beginning; however, it has no explanation as to what caused the "Big Bang." Before the "Big Bang," there was nothing—absolutely nothing, not even a vacuum—and then suddenly there was something. In a fraction of a microsecond, the entire contents of the universe, all of its matter and energy, came exploding out of a point smaller than the head of a pin with a force and intensity we can not even begin to comprehend. If you ask an atheist how and why this happened—how something suddenly come out of nothing—you will not get an answer that comes anywhere near meeting the criteria of the scientific method, nor will you get an answer based on logical argumentation. You will simply hear vague speculation about what may or may not have happened. The atheist has to take it on faith that God did not speak the universe into existence and that the "Big Bang" happened by itself without any encouragement from a higher being.

Given the fact that the atheist does not believe in any kind of "intelligent designer," the atheist must be especially grateful that when matter and energy suddenly came into existence on their very own, they did so in such a way that they behaved in a most orderly way and in accordance with a set of rules. This universe that the atheist says happened by chance turns out to be a very orderly place in which nothing happens by chance! To believe such a paradox could possibly be true takes no small amount of faith.

Similarly, if you ask an atheist how life first began, you should not hold your breath waiting for a clear, scientific description of the process that led to the formation of the first living cells. The explanation you receive will come down to something like this: we know life exists because we are here; we know God didn't create life because we don't believe in God; therefore, somehow a singularity occurred in which just the right conditions were present for life to begin. We don't know what these conditions were, because scientists have never been able to animate inanimate matter. We just have to believe it happened—and that when life just happened, it just so happened in a way that it was pre-programmed to seek nourishment and to reproduce. To believe life would simply come into existence on its own, accidentally programmed to seek nourishment and reproduce, takes great faith. If the first life forms had not been programmed to eat and reproduce, life would have ended with the first generation. Again, the atheist has to be very thankful that in the absence of a Programmer, life was accidentally programmed to do what it needed to do in order to survive.

Atheists also have difficulty explaining the existence of gender. Why are most forms of life made up of male and female members? How did this happen? Geneticists can cite the advantages of a system that requires genetic input from two different contributors. In fact, they will tell you that this system appears to be very well-designed. However, scientists cannot explain exactly how male and female came into existence in the first place. They offer conjectures, but nothing more. Once again, it takes faith to believe something this well-designed was the product of happenstance, especially in the absence of any kind of clear support or explanation from science. It takes great faith to be an atheist.

Indeed, there is much about this very strange species we call *homo sapiens* that one would not expect to see if we lived in a universe comprised of nothing but matter and energy. For example, how does one explain the strange phenomenon we call selfless love? As various people have observed over the years, love makes no sense in a world in which might makes right. Is the existence of love, therefore, evidence that someone created us and left His mark upon us? Or is it just one more absurd coincidence in a universe full of such coincidences?

1

The Fingerprint of God

BEFORE MY FIRST WIFE lost her battle with cancer, we lived in Central Europe for more than twenty years. There we made our home in a country that had languished for forty-five years on the eastern side of the Iron Curtain. During our time of residence in this beautiful country, I taught English in a public secondary school. One of the things I loved about this job was that normally I taught the same students year after year. I would get them when they entered in ninth grade and continue along with them until they graduated or completed their English studies. I got to know many of them quite well (and several continue to be numbered among my friends).

During my students' first year, I made a great effort to get to know these young men and women. I asked a range of simple questions to find out what they were interested in. What kind of music did they listen to (or play)? What were their favorite films? What did they do in their free time? Did they participate in any sports or have favorite teams they cheered for? I then tried to find suitable material related to their interests to bring into the classroom. In this way, I hoped to make the study of English a little less tedious for them.

As the students advanced from the ninth grade through the twelfth and their knowledge of the English language improved, I tried to challenge them with questions of increasing difficulty. I moved from concrete topics to more abstract ones. For example, instead of asking them to describe their best friend, I would ask them to define *friendship*. I would ask my students other questions: Why do humans have a sense of humor? Why do we laugh at the things we laugh at? Why are humans so creative, and why do we put such a high value on various forms of artistic expression? Why is music so important to us? Indeed, modern neurological studies seem to show that the human brain is wired to make and appreciate music and that we actually have a musical intelligence. (That would be a most peculiar development if we were simply the product of happenstance, wouldn't it?)

When the students were in their second year, I would ask how they would behave in a given situation—for example, what would they do if they came upon a wallet that contained a substantial amount of money, as well as an ID, address, and telephone number. Would they keep it or return it? More importantly, what would be the rationale for their behavior?

A little later, I would ask how they knew what was right and what was wrong. What was the basis for their moral and ethical decisions? This was a particularly difficult question to answer for those who held a strictly materialistic view of the universe, for there is no simple way to get around Friedrich Nietzsche's observation that if there is no God, then there is no objective basis for morality. You may disagree with what Hitler or Stalin did, but you cannot say with any objective certainty that they were evil. Words such as *good* and *evil*, *justice* and *injustice* lose their meaning in a universe comprised of nothing but energy and matter. Moral outrage is reduced to a matter of personal preference. Yet humans do, in fact, seem to come equipped with a conscience and an innate sense of morality.

I have two children. I remember how, when they were very young, even before my wife and I had held any deep discussions with them about the impropriety of prevarication, they intuitively knew when they were lying—and they felt guilty about it. We always knew when they weren't telling the truth because they could not look us directly in the eye when they were experiencing veracity malfunctions. Why is that? And why is it that around the globe, and across temporal, cultural, and religious boundaries, certain ethical principles are almost universally accepted as true and valid?

During my students' final year, I would ask where humans had originally come from. Given the fact that I was teaching in a post-Communist, post-modern setting, it was not surprising that many students approached these questions from a materialistic point of view. They began with the assumption that the universe was comprised of nothing but matter and energy. So humans, like other members of the animal kingdom, were believed to be nothing more than the product of a struggle for survival. These students, therefore, would tell me that we lived in a dog-eat-dog world in which big animals ate little animals. We had fought and clawed our way to the top of the food chain and maintained our position there because we were the best at surviving and reproducing. I would nod my head, and we would move on.

Eventually, I would ask what turned out to be the most difficult question of all. I would ask them to give me a definition of love and explain what it was. At first, many of the students considered this an easy assignment. After all, a large proportion of our music, literature, art, and pop culture speaks about love. Indeed, if you turn on the radio right now, you are likely to hear some singer waxing lyrical about the power of love. And if you go to the movies tonight, there is a good chance that love will play a determinative role in driving the plot of whatever film you choose to watch. In the end, however, this question usually turned out to be the most difficult of all to answer. My students found they could not even explain love in their native tongue, much less in English. After all, you cannot hold a certain amount of love in your hand. You cannot measure its length or depth. You cannot weigh it or say what color it is. It is not easy to define such abstractions with mere words. Nevertheless, the class would try. Normally, we would spend the next several lessons trying to come up with a description of what love looked like in practice and then with a working definition of love. The students quickly agreed that the version of "love" peddled by Hollywood and by most purveyors of pop culture was not the real thing. These merchants were selling a counterfeit more akin to infatuation, physical attraction, or simple curiosity. True love was nothing so ephemeral. Rather, it was something that could stand the test of time.

Over the following weeks, students would usually wrestle their way to the conclusion that when you truly love someone, you put that person's needs and interests before your own. They would go on to say that the greatest example of love is laying down one's own life to save that of another. Moreover, they would tell me love was not only something very good, it was also very important—even a basic necessity of life. Love was as important to our existence as oxygen, water, and food because when someone truly believes he, or she, is alone and unloved in this world, that person often ends up the victim of suicide or a patient in a psychiatric hospital. Such a person is unable to function effectively in this world and thus is unlikely to pass along his, or her, DNA.

My students were not the first to observe that humans cannot live in the absence of love. Artists have recognized this fact for centuries—perhaps for millenia. For example, not so long ago W. H. Auden, in his poem "September 1, 1939," spoke for poets and other writers throughout history when he proclaimed, "We must love one another or die."

Nowadays, it is no longer just poets and other artists who speak of the necessity of love. This assertion is supported by science. Recent research in psychology and sociology has shown that loneliness and weak social connections (that is, the absence of love) have the same negative impact on the human lifespan as smoking fifteen cigarettes a day.[1] Even the *Harvard Business Review* has taken note of this fact and in September 2017 devoted several articles to the negative impact loneliness has been shown to have in the workplace.

If we want further evidence of our dire need to be loved, we only have to look as far as the COVID-19 pandemic. If you were to do an internet search on the effects of pandemic-related isolation on people's mental health, you would find dozens of scientific studies on the topic and in a wide array of languages. Around the world in different countries and cultures, observers noted the same phenomenon. As the pandemic dragged on and on, researchers noted a sharp rise in substance abuse, depression, suicide, and other mental health issues. As students were physically separated from their classmates, friends could not gather together socially, people were asked to work from home distant from their colleagues, travel was curtailed, and family members could not see each other on a regular basis, many people increasingly struggled to get through the day. As a species, when we do not experience the love of our friends and family on a regular basis, we generally fail to thrive.

The necessity of love, however, raises a new set of questions. If we live in a dog-eat-dog world in which the strong and powerful are the ones most likely to pass along their genetic material, how could love, which puts the needs and interests of others before its own, have ever come into existence, much less have become a requirement for our existence? Why would the experience of loneliness be just as harmful to me as smoking fifteen cigarettes a day? Other species further down the food chain seem to do just fine without the affection of others of their kind. Of course, it is not hard to see how we can benefit from the love of others, but why would it be a basic condition of our existence? And if love really is unselfish, wouldn't such self-sacrificing behavior reduce the odds of survival of its practitioners? Why then can't we live in the absence of a love that is willing to surrender itself for the sake of others?

---

1. Holt-Lunstad, Smith and Layton, "Social Relationships and Mortality Risk: A Meta-analytic Review," July 27, 2010, https://doi.org/10.1371/journal.pmed.1000316

This is the point where my students struggled to supply answers. In the end, they usually decided they could not explain love. It presented too much of a paradox to resolve. True love did seem to be selfless, but selflessness did not make sense in a world that consisted only of matter and energy and in a world in which the laws of self-preservation and self-propagation governed the progress of species. Love certainly seemed to be real—it even appeared to be a requisite for healthy human existence—but they could not tell me why or where it had come from.

If, in fact, we are little more than a collection of molecules arranged in a complex structure—a structure developed and refined through the process of natural selection—and if through this process we have been programmed to survive and reproduce in a most efficient manner, then the existence (to say nothing of the need) of a selfless "love" that would knowingly lay down its life for the sake of another is . . . nonsensical and confounding. After all, those who act sacrificially are much less likely to pass their genes along to the next generation than are those who put their own survival first. Self-sacrifice runs contrary to the law of survival! It is true that in the wild we may see a mother bear go on the offensive and risk her life to protect her cubs. However, we normally do not see cubs putting their lives in danger to protect the older and weaker members of their species. A majority of my students, however, insisted that they would, in fact, risk their lives to save a grandparent greatly beloved by them.

If humans have such highly developed survival skills and instincts, why would young, intelligent members of our race in the prime of their lives put their precious lives in danger to protect those who are over-the-hill and no longer capable of reproduction? Why risk our lives for someone who is old, ugly, and going to die soon anyway? This kind of behavior just does not make sense in a world that bestows its rewards on survivors.

Moreover, if I have a need to be loved, am I not in some way weaker and more vulnerable than a predator that does not have this same need? If I am feeling depressed because I am lonely and unloved, am I not more likely to serve as the main course at some predator's feast? In fact, I might even save the predator the time and energy and end my life all by myself. Normally, we do not see this kind of self-destructive behavior in the "less-developed" species further down the food chain.

When my students reached the end of their final year, I let them turn the tables on me. During their last month or so, I would let them choose the topics for our discussions and let them ask whatever they wanted to ask.

Inevitably, they would put to me those same tough questions I had once put to them and want to know how I would define love.

When this happened, I would point them to 1 Corinthians 13, where the apostle Paul provided what is perhaps the most famous definition of love. Paul said that love is patient; love is kind and is not jealous. Love does not brag and is not arrogant. It does not seek its own interest. It is not easily provoked, and it does not keep a record of the times it has been offended. Love does not rejoice at unrighteousness. Rather it grieves, and it rejoices in the truth. Love bears all things. Love believes all things. Love sees the best in others and doesn't look for hidden motives and agendas. Love always hopes for the best. Love endures through every trial, and it never fails. In other words, love is more than some nebulous feeling that comes and goes like the weather or that is as fickle as a character in a soap opera. Love—true love—is a decision. It is the decision to put the needs and interests of others before our own. In other words, true love is very much akin to selflessness.

Many would say the opposite of love is hate. But on the basis of 1 Corinthians 13, a good case can be made that the opposite of love is actually selfishness. But if we evolved through a struggle for survival, shouldn't we be the most self-centered species on the planet? Shouldn't all our skills and instincts be honed for self-preservation? I have read arguments that somewhere along the line we developed an "altruistic gene" and became social animals. But it is hard to imagine how that happened. After all, if you are altruistic and I am not, probability favors me outliving you and passing my non-altruistic genes along to the next generation.

My students, therefore, would then want to know, if true love is selfless, where did it come from and why can't we live without it? A materialistic worldview seems incapable of explaining not just the existence of such selflessness but also our need of it. So I would direct my students to 1 John 4. Here John told us not just once, but twice, that God is love. If we then look at the book of Genesis, we read that we were created in the image of God. God said, "Let *us* make man in our own image." So God—the Father, Spirit and Son—created humans as male and female and told them to reproduce. The human family, therefore, was in some way created in the image and likeness of the Trinity. Normally, I avoided any attempt to fathom the depths of trinitarian doctrine with my students. That sort of discussion was above my pay scale. However, I would point out that if, in fact, God is love, and if we were created in the image and likeness of the triune God, we can see why we exist as male and female. This was not the accidental (and inexplicable) by-product of a struggle for survival. It was the intentional reflection of the creative God who, by His very nature, was and is love.

Moreover, if God is love and if He created us in His image, it is not surprising that we need love. We need to love others, and we need to be loved by them. This is the very reason we were created! This is why we exist! Love is our *raison d'être*. We could even say love is God's fingerprint on our lives. It is evidence that He was here and that He created us. It is proof that we are more than just a complex collection of molecules assembled and refined through a struggle for survival.

The mathematician Blaise Pascal noted that we have a deep craving to be loved and this craving has left a great void in our souls. From this, Pascal concluded:

> What else does this craving, and this helplessness, proclaim but that there was once in man a true happiness, of which all that now remains is the empty print and trace? This he tries in vain to fill with everything around him, seeking in things that are not there the help he cannot find in those that are, though none can help, since this infinite abyss can be filled only with an infinite and im-mutable object; in other words by God himself.[2]

There is an emptiness within each of us that can only be filled by the One who made us to love Him. Or, as others have expressed it, God created each of us with a God-shaped hole in our souls that only His love can fill.

One of the best-known verses in the Bible is John 3:16, which says, "For God so loved the world, that He gave His only Son, so that everyone who believes in Him will not perish, but have eternal life." God the Father loves us so much that He gave His very Son as a sacrifice for our sins. Jesus loves us so much that He took on our flesh and endured humiliation, pain, suffering, and physical death so He might ransom us from death. He laid down His life so we might regain ours. This is the greatest example of love the world has ever seen—that the One who spoke the universe into existence laid down His life to save ours. This is love: selflessly putting the needs and desires of others before your own, even at the cost of your own life.

Often when my students thought of Christianity they thought of a set of rules they had to obey, or of a set of procedures or rituals they were required to follow, or perhaps they thought of a set of doctrines they must accept as true. I tried to make the case that if God is love, then the Christian faith is not a set of rules, nor a set of procedures, nor even a set of doctrines.

2. Pascal, *Pensées*, X.148 (428) p. 45.

If God is love, then the Christian faith is a relationship—a personal relationship with our Creator and Savior, a relationship founded on love. This is not to say that doctrine and deeds are unimportant. Rather, it is simply to acknowledge that to be a Christian—a follower of Christ—is first and foremost an act of love. It is to accept the love of the One who made us and to return that love with all of one's heart, mind, soul and strength.

2

The Pattern of the Fingerprint

TWO CARS WERE WAITING at a stoplight. The light turned green, but the elderly woman in the first car didn't notice. The man in the car behind her sat there as the traffic began to whiz around them. Growing impatient, he started beating on his steering wheel and yelling at the woman to step on the gas. The old lady took no notice and continued to sit there. The man became increasingly annoyed. He stuck his head out the window and raised the volume of his voice several decibels while continuing to pound on the steering wheel and dashboard. The lady, however, remained oblivious and sat stationary there in front of the green light. The man then began to blow his car horn. He also held up his index finger so that the woman could see it, and he screamed words out the window you probably would not say in the presence of your grandmother.

The old woman finally looked up in time to see the traffic light change to yellow, so she stepped on the gas and gently accelerated through the intersection just as the light turned red. The man behind her missed his chance to go and had to sit through another red light. He was furious! As he sat there thinking uncharitable thoughts about the elderly woman who had caused this travel delay, he heard a tap on his window. He turned and looked up into the barrel of a gun held by a very serious-looking police officer. The officer told the man to shut off the engine and keep both hands in plain sight. Slowly he did what he was told, in total disbelief of what was happening.

After the man turned the engine off, the officer ordered him to get out of the car with his hands up. The policeman then told the driver to place his hands on the roof of his car. The driver obeyed, and the officer cuffed him and pushed him into the back of the police car. At this point, the man was too shocked to speak. The officer drove him to the police station where he was fingerprinted, photographed, searched, booked, and placed in a cell.

After a couple of hours, another officer led him back to the booking desk where the original officer was waiting with his personal belongings. He returned the items to him and said, "I'm really sorry about this mistake. But you see, I pulled up behind your car while you were blowing your horn, and I saw you giving the finger to the elderly woman in front of you, and I heard you swearing at her. Then I noticed the bumper stickers that said 'What Would Jesus Do?' and 'Follow Me to Sunday School.' I also saw the Christian fish symbol on the back of your car. So, naturally I assumed you had stolen the car."

In this story, there was an incongruence between the behavior the officer witnessed and the behavior he expected given the bumper stickers and Christian symbol he saw on the back of the car. Having come to the conclusion that the true owner of the car was a Christian, he expected to see more charitable behavior from the driver. The policeman may not have been a great theologian, but as a law enforcement official he had learned how to examine a crime scene for clues. One clue that CSI investigators look for is fingerprints.

Every person has a unique set of fingerprints, and each fingerprint has its own individual pattern. So my fingerprints are different from yours. Law enforcement officials are able to use fingerprints to identify suspects when investigators discover prints at the scene of a crime. If we find a certain set of fingerprints on an object, we know the owner of those fingerprints was there. So if love—true love—is the fingerprint of God, if our need for love is proof that God was here and that He left His mark on us, what does His fingerprint look like? What is the pattern of divine love?

Although we may struggle to define love, we do seem to have some idea what it ought to look like in practice. At least, like the officer in the story, we can recognize its absence. Most people also recognize that we need love. They know love is as important to our health and well-being as oxygen, water, and food. Indeed, if one spends any amount of time listening to the radio, watching TV or movies, or reading popular literature, one will quickly discover that almost everybody is talking about love and how to find it. The problem is, although the world recognizes its need for love, it has very little idea what true love really is. (And, like the frustrated driver in the story, even Christians don't always understand the fullness of God's love or do a good job of reflecting it!) Instead of finding true love, the world seems to have been taken in by an assortment of cheap counterfeits. It has been scammed by the Prince of Scammers. Perhaps this is why not too long ago, one hit song simply proclaimed, "Love is a mystery."

C. S. Lewis captured the world's bafflement at love in an amusing way in his book *The Screwtape Letters*. The work comprises the imaginary correspondence between a demon named Wormwood, who is out on assignment, and his immediate superior, a senior demon by the name of Screwtape. At one point, the person whose demise Wormwood has been assigned to effect begins to experience love. This phenomenon completely confuses the clueless demon, so he writes to his more experienced supervisor for advice.

Screwtape, however, finds himself at a loss to explain love. The elder demon confesses he had accidently misspoken when, in previous correspondence, he said that "the Enemy" (God) loved the human vermin. Indeed, anyone could see that what the Enemy calls love is pure nonsense. Given the fact that all selves are by nature in competition, love is a contradiction in terms. Moreover, to say God really loves those wretched creatures would not only be illogical, it would be heresy! Screwtape cautions Wormwood not to breathe a word about this accidental slip of the pen to anyone.

Screwtape claims the reason he made this mistake was because no one in the netherworld has been able to figure out what the Enemy means by love. Everyone knows this so-called selfless love is an impossibility. He, the Enemy, was one being. The humans were distinct from Him. Hence, their good could not possibly be His. Screwtape, therefore, speculates that all the Enemy's talk about love is really just some kind of intentional obfuscation. It is a spiritual slight-of-hand and a form of misdirection. Love, he suggests, is nothing more than a code name for Heaven's secret strategy for defeating the powers of Hell. It is obvious that the Enemy had some ulterior motive for creating the human scum and going to so much trouble on their account. But what could that motive be?

Although the forces of Hell can't figure out what love is, they do recognize it is of the utmost importance. Indeed, members of the Oppressor's faction have freely admitted it. They say if the demons ever came to understand what the Enemy meant by love, the war would be over and the demons would reenter Heaven. So Screwtape concludes this letter by telling Wormwood that Hell is devoting enormous resources to discovering the Enemy's secret. Eventually they will find out what He is really up to and what He means by love. It is obvious He doesn't really love anyone. Nobody does! Love doesn't make sense in a dog-eat-dog world.

Researchers have tested hypothesis after hypothesis, yet they have not been able to unlock the Enemy's secret. Nevertheless, they remain determined to get to the bottom of this mystery. More and more complicated theories will be developed, more and more data will be collected, researchers who make progress will be given greater and greater rewards, while those who fail to do so will be punished with greater and greater severity. This stratagem pursued and accelerated to the very end of time, cannot, surely, fail to succeed.[1]

Like those in Lewis' infernal laboratories, the world around us is also trying to discover what true love really is because deep down inside the world suspects that the meaning of life is to be found in the discovery of love. (As Pascal said, within the human soul there is an infinite abyss that can only be filled by God's love.) But the problem is this: the world doesn't know where to look, nor does it recognize true love when it sees it. Those who listen attentively to what society is saying know the world still hasn't found what it is looking for. The voices of pop culture have much to say about love, but often they confuse love with infatuation and self-gratification. But what can we expect? After all, if one truly believes we live in a dog-eat-dog world, why would one seriously explore the idea of selflessness? There is nothing in it for me—or is there?

When I asked my students to give me a definition of love, they told me it is very difficult to define such an abstract noun. After all, we can't see love. We can't determine what color it is. We can't hold it in our hand and measure its size and weight. We can't take someone to a laboratory, plug the person into a machine, and come up with an objective measurement for love using scientific instrumentation. Nevertheless, love is not entirely invisible. After all, we can see what it looks like when it is put into action!

We have already taken a quick glimpse at the apostle Paul's definition of love in 1 Corinthians 13 (and we will come back to this text). We saw that love appears to be the opposite of self-gratification. True love is a conscious decision to put the needs and desires of another before your own, and the greatest example of love is to give up one's own life to save that of another.

There is yet another way to see what the pattern of love looks like. The Bible tells us the first member of the Trinity often refers to Himself as our "Father." In fact, when Jesus taught His followers to pray, He told them to speak to God as their "father in heaven." When Jesus did this, He told His disciples to use the familiar *Abba* form of father (as opposed to

---

1. Lewis, *The Screwtape Letters*, chapter 19.

the formal). If Jesus had spoken in modern English, He would have told His disciples to speak to their "dad."

So what is a father-child relationship based upon? Unfortunately, we live in a fallen world. As a result, it is not hard to find examples of seriously broken and dysfunctional family relationships. Perhaps some of you are victims of such a relationship and have a hard time thinking kindly of God as some kind of "father." You imagine God in the likeness of your earthly father, who has hurt you in some way. This is understandable. However, we all know the parent-child relationship is one that ought to be based on love—even if that is not always the case in practice. I love my children. (In fact, I think my understanding of love grew immeasurably after the birth of our first child!) I am relatively confident that my children love me. And that is all I really want from them. Knowing that they love me gives me great joy.

My children are now grown and have families of their own. But we still love each other. When they were young (and even now), they could not manipulate me by performing specified rituals or by repeating certain sets of words over and over. I did not require them to master a systematic set of doctrines about me in order for them to be accepted as my children; although, I know that the more they love me the more they will spend time with me and get to know me. I also know that if they love me, they will make it their goal to do those things that give me joy. But this joy comes not so much from the deeds themselves as it does from the love that motivates their deeds.

When my children were growing up, they sometimes made hand-crafted gifts for me that were . . . interesting. (If you have children, perhaps they have done the same for you.) At first glance, it was not always obvious what some of these gifts were meant to be. On more than one occasion, I had to employ subtle powers of reasoning to deduce what a gift was without revealing my ignorance and hurting my child's feelings. Despite the unique and unusual outward form that certain of these offerings assumed, when I recognized they had come from the heart, I treasured them and attached great value to them. Our Father in heaven does the same when we offer up gifts to Him (by way of ourselves and our actions) from our hearts. He is not so much concerned about the exact outward form our offerings might take as He is about the motivation behind the offerings.

When my children were younger and gave me gifts they themselves had made, I was most proud of these gifts. I remember a tie that my daughter once made for me. Even though some people would have scoffed at this tie, looking down on it as a fashion accessory that did not measure up to *GQ* standards and one that under no circumstances should ever be worn on serious or formal occasions, I wore it with pride many times. I even wore it in the pulpit! To me, that tie was evidence of my child's love, and it brought

me joy whenever I had the opportunity to show it off.

This leads us to a point of the utmost importance. It is absolutely critical to understand this and believe it from the bottom of our hearts: God is very pleased with us when we do our best to serve Him from our hearts and when our love for Him is the stimulus to our action. The Bible tells us we have a spiritual adversary, Satan, who is also called the "Accuser" and "Father of Lies." Satan is constantly pointing to our faults and telling us we are undeserving losers. When we try to do something we know will make God happy, Satan laughs at us and tells us our efforts to please God have failed to meet the *GQ* standards. He tells us someone else could have done it better and we wasted our time. He tells us we will have to improve our performace by a significant measure if we ever hope to earn God's love. But Satan is a liar. For one thing, true love is not earned. It is freely given. God loves you because you are His child and not because of anything you may, or may not, have done or said.

God is not always pleased with our behavior. In fact, often our actions and the inclination of our hearts cause Him pain, but this does not diminsh His love for us. Indeed, the gifts and offerings we make to Him because of a heartfelt love give Him great joy. In the same way that I would wear my daughter's tie and show it off, I can imagine God taking our gifts and showing them off to the heavenly hosts, saying, "Look here, everybody, see what my precious child did for me today. Isn't this a work of beauty?"

In 1 John 4:17-18, John refers to the Day of Judgment: "By this, love is perfected with us, so that we may have confidence in the day of judgment; because as He is, we also are in this world. There is no fear in love, but perfect love drives out fear, because fear involves punishment, and the one who fears is not perfected in love."

In many places, Scripture tells us that a Day of Judgment is coming when each of us will have to give account for all of our actions. This fact used to scare me because I knew (as I still know) that I was far from perfect. John, however, says that "we may have confidence in the day of judgment." Those who love God will have nothing to fear on that day, for there is no fear in love. Take note of this! According to John, what is going to be important on Judgment Day? Love! On that day, the Lord is not going to ask us whether we were baptized as infants or as adults. He is not going to ask whether we were sprinkled or immersed. He is not going to ask our opinion on the millennium. He is not going to ask which theologian we followed or which ecclesiastical tradition we belonged to. He is not going to ask if we prefered traditional or contemporary church music. He is not going to ask us about any of these issues that we, His squabbling children, spend so much time arguing over. Rather, on the Day of Judgment the Lord will have two simple questions for each of us. As He extends His nail-scarred hands, He will simply ask, "Do you love me?" and "Did others see me through you?" Did the world see my fingerprint on your life? Who came to know me because of you?

Lord, You have searched me and known me.
You know when I sit down and when I get up;
You understand my thought from far away.
You scrutinize my path and my lying down,
And are acquainted with all my ways.
Even before there is a word on my tongue,
Behold, Lord, You know it all.
You have encircled me behind and in front,
And placed Your hand upon me.
Such knowledge is too wonderful for me;
It is too high, I cannot comprehend it.

Where can I go from Your Spirit?
Or where can I flee from Your presence?
If I ascend to heaven, You are there;
If I make my bed in Sheol, behold, You are there.
If I take up the wings of the dawn,
If I dwell in the remotest part of the sea,
Even there Your hand will lead me,
And Your right hand will take hold of me.
If I say, "Surely the darkness will overwhelm me,
And the light around me will be night,"
Even darkness is not dark to You,
And the night is as bright as the day.
Darkness and light are alike to You.
For You created my innermost parts;
You wove me in my mother's womb.
I will give thanks to You, because I am awesomely and wonderfully made;
Wonderful are Your works,
And my soul knows it very well.
My frame was not hidden from You
When I was made in secret,
And skillfully formed in the depths of the earth;
Your eyes have seen my formless substance;
And in Your book were written
All the days that were ordained for me,
When as yet there was not one of them.
How precious also are Your thoughts for me, God!
How vast is the sum of them!
Were I to count them, they would outnumber the sand.
When I awake, I am still with You.

—Psalm 139 1-18

3

The God Who Is Here

'I will also walk among you and be your God,
and you shall be My people.'

—Leviticus 26:12

MORE THAN SEVEN HUNDRED years before Jesus was born, Ahaz ruled over the Kingdom of Judah, and according to the books of 2 Kings and Isaiah, he did evil in the sight of the Lord. In chapter 7 of Isaiah, it was reported that the kings of Israel and Aram marched against Judah and laid siege to Jerusalem. When news of the impending attack reached Ahaz, Scripture tells us that "the hearts of the people shook as trees in the forest shaken by the wind."

Despite the wickedness of Ahaz, the Lord did not forget the promises He had made to His people at different times in history. So He sent the prophet Isaiah to Ahaz with a message of comfort. At least, it was a message that contained some comfort. God was still going to discipline Ahaz and the people of Judah for their sin. Hard times were coming, and there would be no escape. However, the Lord promised that the lands of Judah's adversaries, Israel and Aram, would eventually be forsaken and the House of David would one day be restored. As a sign of this promise, God said, "Behold, the virgin will conceive and give birth to a son, and she will name him Immanuel" (Isaiah 7:14).

The Gospel of Matthew tells us of the birth of this child just over seven hundred years later. The child was Jesus. The name *Jesus* is the Aramaic version of the name *Joshua*. The name *Joshua* means "the Lord (or Jehovah) is salvation." Jesus was also called *Immanuel*, which means "God with us." These are two most interesting and significant names: *God with us* and the

Lord is our salvation. Jesus quite literally is God with us, and His presence with us is evidence that the Lord is our salvation.

Christians in the West celebrate the birth of Jesus, the Christ, on December 25. Christians in many eastern countries celebrate His birth on January 7. In both regions, the period leading up to this celebration is known as Advent. The word *Advent* is derived from the Latin verb *advenire*, which means "to come" or "to arrive," and it means *arrival*. Advent is the time of year when Christians prepare for the arrival of God's son Jesus, who came, took on our flesh, and lived here with us. The incarnation of Jesus Christ, then, is something that sets the Christian faith in stark contrast to all the other religions of the world.

There are, in fact, many religions in the world today. Except for atheism, all of these religions believe in the existence of some sort of divine being. Therefore, most religions claim they can tell us something about God. They claim that they can tell us how and where we can find God, and then how we can earn our salvation. If one were to examine these different religions closely, one would find that with just one great exception all the religions teach their followers that God is somewhere out there, and it is our responsibility first to go out and find Him and then to earn His pleasure. With just one exception, every other religion tells us we are playing some sort of game of cosmic hide-and-seek in which God is concealed out in the universe and it is our task to discover where He is and to win His approval through our good behavior.

For example, both Buddhism and Hinduism tell their followers that the quest for salvation is a long and arduous one that takes place over the course of many lifetimes. If a person does well in one lifetime, that person will then assume a higher form of life upon reincarnation. Correspondingly, one will move downward if one does not live up to divine standards. The goal is to continue ascending until one's soul finally merges with the divine.

Muslims teach that you must follow with unquestioning obedience the laws that God handed down to the prophet Mohammed in the Koran. If you can live up to this divine standard, God might let you into heaven when you pass from this life into the next. But it is very much up to you to work your way into God's favor.

The New Age movement encompasses a wide range of beliefs and practices. However, it is not uncommon within the New Age movement to find teachers who tell you that you need a spiritual guide to help you navigate the spiritual realm. Otherwise, as an earth-bound and uneducated resident of the physical realm, you will never find God on your own.

We could look at other religions, as well, and we could go into greater depth with each one. But you will find that with just one exception every other religion—at least all those that I have ever encountered—tells us that God, in one way or another, is hidden and that it is up to us to find Him and make our way to Him. We are responsible for earning our own salvation; therefore, we must make the first move toward God.

The one great exception is Christianity. Unlike other religions that ask us to play a game of cosmic hide-and-seek, Christianity tells us that Jesus, God's Son, the second person of the Trinity, left the glory He enjoyed in heaven and came to earth to find us. Christianity tells us that God is not an impersonal force; rather He is a person—actually three persons: Father, Holy Spirit, and Son. Moreover, Christianity tells us that God loves us. He loves us so much that even when we turned our backs on Him and chose to follow the path of selfishness, Jesus pursued us to win us back with His love and His selflessness. This, in fact, is what Christmas is all about. It is the account of how God came to find and save us, and it is a very important chapter in the divine love story.

Christmas is so much more than the celebration of materialism that our modern world has turned it into! However, to fully comprehend and appreciate what Christmas is all about, we need to know more about who Jesus is. Why is it so astounding that He became one of us? Who was He, and what makes His birth so very special? As Scripture tells us, He is "God with us." He is the God who is here. Jesus is the God who left Heaven to seek and save us. And He did this even before we knew that we were lost. He didn't wait for us to make the first move or to work our way into His favor.

This sounds quite grand, doesn't it? But maybe you are like me, and sometimes you have a hard time really getting your mind around ideas like these that are simply too big for our human words to hold. Maybe you need a picture to give your mind something to grasp onto and that will help put some substance to these words? Who is this Jesus who was born in a stable and laid in that manger just over 2000 years ago? And why was His birth so amazing?

The Gospel of John begins by introducing Jesus to us as follows: "In the beginning was the Word, and the Word was with God, and the Word was God. He was in the beginning with God. All things came into being through Him, and apart from Him not even one thing came into being that has come into being." (John 1:1-3) John makes it clear in his writing that Jesus is the "Word of God." In Colossians 1:15-17, the apostle Paul writes that Jesus "is the image of the invisible God, the firstborn of all creation: for by Him all things were created, both in the heavens and on earth, visible and invisible, whether thrones, or dominions, or rulers, or authorities—all things have been created through Him and for Him. He is before all things, and in Him all things hold together." In other words, Jesus is the one who created the universe. He is the one who spoke and who brought all things into existence.

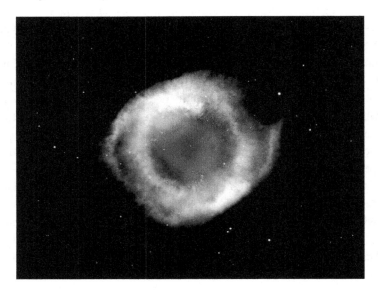

Hold that thought for a moment. This photo is one NASA produced using data received by the Hubble space telescope. This is a picture of the Helix Nebula. Its technical designation is NGC 7293, however, it has been nicknamed "the Eye of God."[1] You can probably guess why. Astrophysicists tell us this nebula spans a distance of 2.5 light years. A light year, as you probably know, is the distance light travels in one year, approximately 5.88 trillion miles. So 2.5 light years would be about 14.7 trillion miles. How far is that? Well, let's say you lived to the ripe old age of a hundred. You would be alive and breathing for 36,525 days (taking into account leap years). That would be 876,600 hours, or 52,596,000

1. If you would like to see what this nebula looks like in full color (and I highly recommend that you do), go to <https://apod.nasa.gov/apod/apo30510.html>.

minutes, or 3,155,760,000 seconds. So in order for you to travel from one side of this nebula to the other during your lifetime, you would have to travel over 4,658 miles every second of your life! That is farther than the distance from Boston to Anchorage. And you would have to cover that distance every single second for one hundred years.

When I had a chance to visit my brother in Alaska a few summers ago, I thought it was the most magnificent place I had ever seen. On many occasions, I found myself in complete awe of God's creation. But Alaska is nothing compared to this nebula. Now think about this: astronomers estimate that the universe is made up of trillions of other celestial bodies of various kinds. So if you were to name one of these bodies per second during your hundred-year journey from one side of NGC 7293 to the other, you still would not be able to name all the bodies that are out there. We simply lack the words to describe the majesty of the universe. Does this give you some sense of how great and awesome our God and creator is? Jesus is the one who created all this and who holds it together by the power of His word. And Christmas is the celebration of how He set aside His glory, of how He emptied Himself, came to Earth, and became one of us in order to find and save us.

Now, because Jesus came and found us and because He has accomplished all that was necessary for our salvation, we no longer have to play hide-and-seek with God. We don't have to climb the peaks of Nepal looking for truth. We no longer have to escape to the desert to try to achieve spiritual perfection. We no longer have to practice exotic forms of meditation, mysticism, asceticism, or other so-called forms of spiritual exercises in order to win God's approval. We don't need spiritual guides to find God, and we don't need to work out our salvation over the course of many lifetimes as we are reincarnated over and over. We don't have to go out and find God, because God has already found us. We simply need to recognize who Jesus is, believe in Him, love Him, and then follow after Him.

About seven centuries before the birth of Jesus, God spoke through the prophet Isaiah and said, "Therefore the Lord Himself will give you a sign: Behold, the virgin will conceive and give birth to a son, and she will name Him Immanuel." We can then read in the Gospel of Matthew 1:18-25:

> Now the birth of Jesus the Messiah was as follows: when His mother Mary had been betrothed to Joseph, before they came together she was found to be pregnant by the Holy Spirit. And her husband Joseph, since he was a righteous man and did not want

to disgrace her, planned to send her away secretly. But when he had thought this over, behold, an angel of the Lord appeared to him in a dream, saying, "Joseph, son of David, do not be afraid to take Mary as your wife; for the Child who has been conceived in her is of the Holy Spirit. She will give birth to a Son; and you shall name Him Jesus, for He will save His people from their sins." Now all this took place so that what was spoken by the Lord through the prophet would be fulfilled: "Behold, the virgin will conceive and give birth to a Son, and they shall name Him Immanuel," which translated means, "God with us." And Joseph awoke from his sleep and did as the angel of the Lord commanded him, and took Mary as his wife, but kept her a virgin until she gave birth to a Son; and he named Him Jesus."

Jesus is God with us. He is the Lord, and He is our salvation.

Some of you, perhaps, have read C. S. Lewis's wonderful tale *The Lion, the Witch and the Wardrobe,* or you might have seen the film based on this story. I am not going to summarize the whole plot for you—no spoilers for those who have yet to read the book. Nevertheless, I can tell you it is a tale of four children who stumbled through a magical wardrobe and found themselves in a land called Narnia. When the youngest girl, Lucy, first arrived, she met a fawn who told her about Narnia and about the White Witch, who along with her evil army had conquered Narnia. The White Witch had plunged the entire land into a deep winter in which there was no Christmas. "Always winter and never Christmas; think of that!" said the fawn. Lucy responded, "How awful!" And so it would be awful if we didn't have Christmas. It would be awful if Jesus had never been born or if He had never died and then risen! Think of it. We would still be searching blindly for truth. We would still be without hope of salvation. We would still be playing that great cosmic game of hide-and-seek for God.

Jesus, however, was indeed born, and we do have Christmas. A little more than two thousand years ago in the otherwise obscure town of Bethlehem, Mary gave birth to Jesus and laid him to rest in a manger. In contrast with all of the other religions of this world that tell us we somehow must find God, Christianity announces the good news that God found us. While we were yet sinners, while we were still in rebellion against God and were separated from Him by our sin, He became one of us. In contrast to those religions that tell us God is impersonal, or that He doesn't care, or that He is only a vengeful judge, or that He is some mysterious life force, Christianity affirms the fact that God is personal and that He loves us with a mad, passionate love so wide and so deep we cannot fully understand it. God loves us so much that even when we turned our backs on Him, when we left Him to go our own way, He pursued us; He came after us. He pursued us to the very gates of Sheol to save us from our sins. As it says in the Gospel of John 3:16-17: "For God so loved the world, that He gave His only Son, so that everyone who believes in Him will not perish, but have eternal life. For God did not send the Son into the world to judge the world, but so that the world might be saved through Him."

As Christians, what difference should all this make in our lives? If we say we believe in Jesus Christ and we accept the sacrifice He made on our behalf, should it have any effect on the way we live our lives? Should it make any difference that Jesus was born of Mary, that He took on our flesh, and that He is now with us? The answer is yes.

Consider what Paul said when he wrote to the Christians in Phillipi (Philippians 2:5-8): "Have this attitude in yourselves which was also in Christ Jesus, who, as He already existed in the form of God, did not consider equality with God something to be grasped, but emptied Himself by taking the form of a bond-servant and being born in the likeness of men. And being found in appearance as a man, He humbled Himself by becoming obedient to the point of death: death on a cross." Jesus emptied Himself, He made Himself nothing, and He became a servant. Paul tells us that as His followers, we are to have the same attitude. We are also to be humble servants.

Do you remember how Jesus spent His time on earth, whom He talked to, whom He ate with? Jesus came into this world and spent most of His time not with those who thought themselves righteous but with those who recognized that they were truly sinners. He spent much of His time with the outcasts of society: with the poor, with the lepers, with the tax gatherers and prostitutes. He didn't just hang out with the wealthy and powerful, or even with the "good"— although He did spend some time with them, too.

There used to be a TV program called "Lifestyles of the Rich and Famous." Each week the host would interview some fabulously wealthy person and show something of the luxurious life this person lived. I don't think the host of this show would ever have bothered interviewing Jesus because, according to the world's standards, He was not rich and famous.

When Jesus came into the world, He walked among us and He walked with us. And that is what we are now called upon to do. Scripture refers to the Church—that is all of us who are followers of Christ—as Christ's Body and as the temple and the dwelling place of the Holy Spirit. This Body has been called upon to live in the midst of the world, and it has been given the task of bringing the good news of Jesus Christ to those still living in the darkness, to those still searching the cosmos trying to find God and still prisoners of their own selfishness. We are told not to isolate, or insulate, ourselves from the world; rather, we are to live and work right in the midst of the world—and in so doing, we are to transform the world. As those around us are looking for meaning in the stars or in altered states of consciousness or on top of Mount Everest or within the confines of their own soul, we are called upon to be a light, to be the salt of the earth, to tell them God is not way out there somewhere, that God is not some impersonal force but a personal God who loves us, that He has walked among us, and that He is here. We are to point to Jesus Christ, Immanuel, God with us.

Around 350 years ago, George Herbert wrote a poem entitled "Redemption." In many ways, this short poem captures the inexpressible wonder of God's love and His humility. It goes to the heart of what it meant for Jesus to leave His heavenly home to come and be with us here on earth as Immanuel.

Redemption

Having been tenant long to a rich lord,
   Not thriving, I resolved to be bold,
   And to make a suit unto him, to afford
A new small-rented lease, and cancell th'old.

In heaven at his manor I him sought:
   They told me there that he was lately gone
   About some land, which he had dearly bought
Long since on earth, to take possession.

I straight return'd, and knowing his great birth,
   Sought him accordingly in great resorts;
   In cities, theaters, gardens, parks, and courts:
At length I heard a ragged noise and mirth

   Of thieves and murderers; there I him espied,
   Who straight, *Your suit is granted*, said, and died.

—*George Herbert (1593-1633)*

4

What Child Is This?

THIS PICTURE IS A fairly typical medieval representation of Mary and the infant Jesus.[1] Does anything strike you about the way Jesus was portrayed—other than the fact that He has a 5-o'clock shadow and looks a lot like a gangster from a 1940s film? Except for the fact that He is so small, He looks older than His mother, doesn't He? I have two children, and neither of them as babies ever did that "papal blessing" thing with the two fingers on their right hands. Normal human infants just don't do that sort of thing.

1. *Madonna and Child with Two Angels* by Matteo di Giovanni (1482) in the permanent collection of the Keresztény Múzeum in Esztergom, Hungary. You can see the picture in full color at <http://www.keresztenymuzeum.hu/gallery/orig/33_0.jpg >.

In this picture, and in hundreds of others like it, we see Jesus portrayed as a baby but not really as a normal human child. He is still very much the Lord of the universe. He is simply dressed up in the skin of a human infant as if He were wearing a masquerade costume. It is as though He were a visitor from heaven, disguised as a child but still in complete command of all creation.

At the time of the early church, Jesus was most often portrayed as the Good Shepherd who had come to find His lost sheep.[2] Quite often, He was also shown sitting around a table and breaking bread with His followers. But slowly, over the course of a thousand years or so, He was separated from those He had come to save and put way up high on a judgment seat over the entrance of the church, or even higher up in the dome over the sanctuary. In fact, so much distance was put between Him and us, we

2. For example, the picture you see here is of a 3rd Century fresco found in the catacomb of Priscilla on the Via Salaria in Rome.

started to need the help of Mary and the other saints to approach Him. Eventually, we couldn't even share His meal with Him any more, because the priests were afraid we would desecrate it. The clergy drank the wine on our behalf, and they placed the "bread" directly on our tongues so we wouldn't do something unholy to it by accident.

The human mind, limited as it is, has a very hard time comprehending how Jesus could be both fully divine and fully human at the same time. It tends to emphasize one to the exclusion of the other. For example, in our picture, the artist imagined Jesus as human in form only. Behind the 5-o'clock shadow, the second person of the Trinity was still omnipotent and omniscient. But, in truth, when Jesus was born in Bethlehem two thousand and some years ago, the second person of the Trinity became as fully human as you and I. And in doing so, He became as limited by His humanity as you and I are.

He set aside His power and His glory to the point that He required His parents to clean Him up when He dirtied Himself. He was dependent upon them to feed Him when He was hungry. He was not playacting or wearing a masquerade costume. He truly was a human infant, and He was limited by His humanity.

Luke 2:41-52 gives us some helpful insight into what it meant for Jesus to be fully human:

> His (Jesus') parents went to Jerusalem every year at the Feast of the Passover. And when He was twelve years old, they went up there according to the custom of the feast; and as they were returning, after spending the full number of days required, the boy Jesus stayed behind in Jerusalem, but His parents were unaware of it. Instead, they thought that He was somewhere in the caravan, and they went a day's journey, and then they began looking for Him among their relatives and acquaintances. And when they did not find Him, they returned to Jerusalem to look for Him.
>
> Then, after three days they found Him in the temple, sitting in the midst of the teachers, both listening to them and asking them questions. And all who heard Him were amazed at His understanding and His answers. When Jospeh and Mary saw Him, they were bewildered; and His mother said to Him, "Son, why have You treated us this way? Behold, Your father and I have been anxiously looking for You!"
>
> And He said to them, "Why is it that you were looking for Me? Did you not know that I had to be in My Father's house?" And yet they on their part did not understand the statement which

He had made to them. And He then went down with them and came to Nazareth, and He continued to be subject to them; and His mother treasured all these things in her heart.

And Jesus kept increasing in wisdom and stature, and in favor with God and people.

This passage more or less tells us everything we know about Jesus' childhood. Matthew and Luke tell us a little bit about the circumstances surrounding Jesus' birth, but except for this story, we don't know anything else about Jesus' life until He begins His ministry at the age of thirty. So we might want to consider why this one particular incident was recorded. What is God telling us here?

Until recently, I thought this seemingly straight-forward story was meant simply to provide another example of Jesus' wisdom and authority—which it does. Here we see a twelve-year-old boy sitting in the temple in Jerusalem conversing with the greatest biblical scholars in Israel, and all who heard Him were amazed by His understanding of God's Word. In my previous and cursory reading of this text, I supposed Jesus was doing the teaching and the scholars were asking the questions.

Joseph and Mary, of course, knew their child was special, but it doesn't appear at this point that they fully comprehended just how special and unique Jesus was. Indeed, they seemed quite mystified by His behavior. Verse 48 records Mary asking, "Son, why have You treated us this way? Behold, Your father and I have been anxiously looking for You!" I used to think this text just showed how otherworldly Jesus was and that He had wisdom and insight beyond His years. For a long time, I thought that was all the story was put there to tell us. I more or less pictured Jesus like the Jesus in the medieval painting—Master of the Universe dressed up as a human child.

Not long ago, however, I noticed something in verses 51 and 52 I hadn't seen before. Luke tells us that after Jesus left the temple, He returned to Nazareth with Joseph and Mary and continued to be subject to them. That is, He continued to obey them. Luke also says Jesus continued to grow in wisdom.

I always knew that Jesus was obedient. However, I had associated His obedience with the obedience He had shown to His Heavenly Father. I had never really thought about Him placing Himself in subjection to lowly humans—except when it was time for Him to die and He allowed the authorities to crucify Him. But this passage shows that Jesus continued to obey Joseph and Mary.

Think about this: Jesus, the Word of God, was sitting in the temple discussing Scripture with some of the greatest minds in Israel, but when His mom and dad came looking for Him and told Him to come home, He said, "Okay" and obeyed them. The second person of the Trinity who had created all things, who had spoken and the universe had come into existence, who had created the distant galaxies (along with NGC 7293, the Helix Nebula) and all the living things you see around you, who had even, in some way, had had a hand in creating Joseph and Mary, put Himself in subjection to these two fallen creatures. We need to understand the implications of this critically important point.

What is God trying to show us and teach us through this example? Jesus, being God, knew more than His parents. There must have been many times when Joseph and Mary, like all normal, fallen human beings, made mistakes or even sinned and when Jesus could have corrected them. But the Bible says He obeyed them. I know that the Catholic Church believes that Mary never had any other children. However, there are several places in Scripture that mention Jesus' brothers. Perhaps Joseph was a widower when he took Mary as his wife and had older children from his prior marriage. Assuming Jesus did have siblings (regardless of who their biological mother was), do you think that when Joseph or Mary made a mistake or a bad decision, Jesus started pointing out the error of their ways to His brothers? Do you think He started second-guessing His parents in front of His brothers, saying things like, "Well, if I were them, I would have done such and such"? I don't think so.

If Jesus had undermined the authority of His parents, what would that have done to them and their ability to raise a family? What would it have done to His siblings? By keeping silent and obeying, Jesus allowed Joseph and Mary to mature as parents. He allowed His siblings to learn to respect His parents and their authority. Sometimes we need to give others the freedom to make mistakes so God can use these mistakes to help them mature, and sometimes this is more important in the long run than whether or not we are right. At other times, God is trying to teach *us* something. Sometimes it is more important to God that we learn humility and obedience than it is for us to know the "right" answer. If Jesus was willing to place Himself in subjection to those fallen humans His Father had placed in authority, then how important is it for us to do the same?

Now look again at verse 52. Luke tells us, "Jesus kept increasing in wisdom and stature, and in favor with God and people." I used to think Jesus was already full of wisdom. But as I began to investigate what Scripture said about His humanity, I started to suspect that when Jesus became one of us, He limited Himself in this area as well. As you read this text in Luke, you will see He was not teaching the people in the temple. Rather, He was listening to the scholars and asking questions. He was trying to learn from those who knew more than He did. He had wisdom and maturity beyond His years, but He was limited in what He knew.

In Philippians 2:5-8, Paul wrote, "Have this attitude in yourselves which was also in Christ Jesus, who, as He already existed in the form of God, did not consider equality with God something to be grasped, but emptied Himself by taking the form of a bond-servant and being born in the likeness of men. And being found in appearance as a man, He humbled Himself by becoming obedient to the point of death: death on a cross." Just what does this mean?

When I was in college, I was in a weekly Bible study, and the members of the group all decided they would volunteer at a local nursing home. We would each go over there one night a week and talk to the patients or help feed them—whatever needed to be done. One evening, I was feeding an elderly gentleman who had had a stroke. He was a retired professor who had once taught at an Ivy League institution. He seemed quite elegant and dignified, but while he was eating, he lost control of himself and he soiled his trousers. I quickly alerted the nursing home staff so they could attend to him. He didn't say anything, but I noticed as they were wheeling him back into his room that tears had started to roll down the side of his face. I am guessing that he felt humiliated by what he had done. Imagine how mortifying it must have been for this man—once a respected member of the academic community known for his intellectual prowess and abilities—to be unable to control himself and have to rely on others to undress and clean him up.

Which of us would willingly suffer this kind of humiliation? Who would volunteer to do this? Most of us dread the day when we might find ourselves in the same humbling situation. We pray we are never reduced to such a demeaning state of helplessness, don't we?

When Isaiah foretold the coming of the Messiah, he said the Savior's name would be "Wonderful Counselor, Mighty God, Eternal Father, Prince of Peace." This is who Jesus is: Wonderful Counselor, Mighty God, Eternal

Father, Prince of Peace! This is a far more exalted position than university professor. Nevertheless, Jesus voluntarily emptied Himself—to the extent that He required Joseph and Mary to clean Him when He dirtied Himself and that he depended on them to feed Him when He was hungry.

When Jesus was born and laid to rest in that manger, He was not play-acting. Paul wrote that Jesus had completely emptied Himself. Jesus put Himself in subjection to human parents, and He obeyed them—even when they were wrong or made mistakes. Even His knowledge was restricted by His humanity, since as He grew older He also grew in wisdom.

None of us have anywhere near the power and the glory our Creator does. Yet, we break down and weep when we experience the type of humiliation the elderly professor experienced, don't we? It is agonizing and painful on several levels. Certainly we would not seek out or volunteer for such an experience; we have too much pride. So why did Jesus, the second person of the Trinity, the Word of God, humble Himself to such a degree that He became one of us—a helpless infant who needed to be cleaned and fed and subject to the will of His parents?

The simple answer to this question is love. Jesus loves us so much He was willing to endure this kind of humiliation, in order to be able to spend all eternity with us. If this was what was required for Him to break the power that sin and death had gained over us, then this was the degree to which He would humble Himself.

But in doing this Jesus not only set us free from the power of sin, but He also gave us an example to follow. As Paul wrote in Philippians, we are to have this same attitude in ourselves that was also in Christ Jesus, who although He existed in the form of God, did not regard equality with God a thing to be grasped, but emptied Himself.

A few years back, I was meeting with a group of missionaries from around the world. As we talked about various congregations we knew of back in our home countries—the U.S., Canada, Great Britain, and New Zealand—we were dismayed to find that each of us had personal knowledge of at least one sizable congregation in the process of a divisive split. Why were these churches splitting? Within each of those congregations there were people more concerned with being "right" about some particular issue (style of worship, method of baptism, a church building project, etc.) than in following Christ's example of humility and obedience.

Perhaps such local squabbles seem insignificant when looking at the global picture, but when these congregations fragmented and broke apart, the Church as a whole around the world was weakened. These congregations became weaker and less able to support foreign missions; they also withdrew from local evangelistic efforts. Families were hurt and left the Church—some for good. Some of the children from these families took in a harsh, negative view of God's Kingdom. They walked away and never looked back. However, I have also seen that when God's people have replaced the spirit of criticism with the spirit of humility, and when they have set their own agendas aside and have begun to work together for the glory of God, when they have submitted to one another and obeyed one another, truly amazing things have happened.

Jesus loves you. He loves you so much that He emptied Himself for you. He endured humiliation of a greater magnitude than we will ever know. In Romans 8, the apostle Paul tells us that Jesus loves us so much that neither height nor depth, nor angels nor principalities, nor anything in heaven or on earth, not even death can separate us from His love.

We are Christ's people, His followers, and He wants us to follow His example. If He, very God of very God, was willing to endure this kind of humiliation, then what must we do? Imagine you met someone who had been born blind and had never ever seen color of any kind. Suppose the two of you are sitting and talking while you watch a beautiful sunset. As the sun slowly sinks below the horizon, you start describing the fiery reds and purples you see painting the sky. The blind person asks, "What is this red you speak of? What is purple?" How would you explain the color red to someone who had never seen it? You could give your friend a scientific or mathematical definition of red: "Well, the color red is a form of electromagnetic energy between the wavelength of 700 nm and the wavelength of 400 nm." You might proffer the mathematical equation of light. Your friend might gain some abstract knowledge of the color red, but he would still not know what you know. The person would not be able to imagine that sunset you are experiencing or be able to comprehend the fullness of red the way you do.

$$\nabla \cdot \mathbf{D} = \rho$$

$$\nabla \cdot \mathbf{B} = 0$$

$$\nabla \times \mathbf{E} = -\frac{\partial \mathbf{B}}{\partial t}$$

$$\nabla \times \mathbf{H} = \frac{\partial \mathbf{D}}{\partial t} + \mathbf{J}$$

As Christians, we talk a lot about love. But is it just a theory? Is it like a mathematical formula? If somebody doesn't know what true love is, how are they going to find out? It is not through our words but through our actions. We have to help them experience it firsthand. To do this, we have got to lay down our lives for them. We live in a broken world. Christ allowed Himself to be broken for us, and that is what He wants us to do for the world. To bring the Good News of what He has done for us, we need to allow ourselves to be broken as well.

In Galatians 5:13, Paul tells us we have been set free from sin. Our Lord has freed you from the bondage that sin and death formerly had over you. But don't use your freedom for selfish purposes. Take this freedom now and use it to serve one another in love.

When I Survey the Wondrous Cross

When I survey the wondrous cross
On which the Prince of glory died,
My richest gain I count but loss,
And pour contempt on all my pride.

Forbid it, Lord, that I should boast,
Save in the death of Christ my God!
All the vain things that charm me most,
I sacrifice them to His blood.

See from His head, His hands, His feet,
Sorrow and love flow mingled down!
Did e'er such love and sorrow meet,
Or thorns compose so rich a crown?

Were the whole realm of nature mine,
That were a present far too small;
Love so amazing, so divine,
Demands my soul, my life, my all.

—*Isaac Watts (1674-1748)*

5

Humility: What's Love Got to Do with It?

When pride comes, then comes dishonor;
But with the humble there is wisdom.

—Proverbs 11:2

Pride goes before destruction, and
a haughty spirit before stumbling."

—Proverbs 16:18

Clothe yourselves with humility toward one another, because
God is opposed to the proud, but He gives grace to the humble.
Therefore humble yourselves under the mighty hand of God, so
that He may exalt you at the proper time, having cast all your
anxiety on Him, because He cares about you.

—1 Peter 5:5-7

THESE TEXTS SPEAK OF pride and humility, two traits that call for closer examination. The problem is, true humility is often a difficult quality to recognize. But don't worry! I have discovered the secret of humility and will be shedding full light on the subject in my forthcoming book, *Humility and How I Attained It.* The book will come with a life-size portrait of me (drawn by my grandson) being humble so that you can see what true humility looks like. This volume will be in bookstores soon, and once it is on the shelves I will make myself available to autograph copies of the book.

PAPA

Obviously, I'm kidding. I have a long, long way to go to master the virtue of humility. This illustration, however, demonstrates how difficult it can be to recognize this allusive virtue, for there is something about genuine humility that doesn't draw attention to itself. Humility frequently goes unnoticed. What, then, is true humility? In the simplest terms, true humility is right thinking about ourselves. It is seeing ourselves, and accepting ourselves, as we really are—as no better, but also no worse, no more or no less wonderful than God has made us.

On the one hand, humility recognizes its sins and weaknesses. It admits it is not perfect, that it does not know everything, and that it depends on God's grace. Humility, therefore, constantly looks to the Lord for mercy, strength, and guidance. Because humility knows it is not perfect, it doesn't stand in judgment over others; rather, it is patient and forgiving because it knows just how much it depends on God's patience and forgiveness.

Over the years, I have had students who thought they already knew everything they needed to know about the English language. Some of those students were quite intelligent, but they were foolish! They were foolish because pride prevented them from learning anything new.

When I was young, my grandfather had a wonderful woodshop. He was a medical doctor, but his hobby was woodworking. He fashioned some beautiful works of art in that shop of his. He also guarded that shop assiduously, keeping it under lock and key. He allowed access only to a small number of trusted people. He didn't want some uninitiated clod messing with his precious tools. One day he invited me into this protected sanctum. He said he was going to teach me how to use some of the tools and help me build a bird house. I felt honored, not to mention excited. Grampa got down the first tool and started to explain what it was for and how to use it. But before he could finish his words of instruction, I said, "I know!" So he put the tool back, and we moved on to the next piece of equipment. Again he started to tell me what it was for and how to handle it. Once again before he could finish, I said, "I know!" When this little scenario played itself out again at the third stop on my tour, my grandfather looked me in the eye and said very gently but with some sadness, "I guess if you already know everything, then there really isn't anything I can teach you here." I suddenly felt embarrassed. I learned something important that day that was not in the original lesson plan: humility is aware that it still has much to learn. It recognizes its faults and weaknesses.

Humility, on the other hand, does not go around telling everyone how worthless, pathetic and miserable it is. Perhaps you have seen the film *Notting Hill*? There is a scene in this film in which the characters sit around a table and have a competition to see who has lived the most miserable life. Some people may think this is humility, but it is not. This is false humility, and it is really just another form of pride. Contests like this are simply alternative means of drawing attention to ourselves.

True humility does not hide its gifts and talents behind a mask of helplessness and self-pity. This kind of behavior is false humility. You may recall that Moses once tried this tactic. When God sent him to speak to Pharaoh, Moses argued that he was the wrong man for the job. He said he wasn't qualified for this task because he was not a good speaker. How did God respond to such protestations? God already knew what Moses was capable of. God knew Moses was not a gifted orator. In fact, that is one of the reasons God chose Moses for the job. God planned to be his strength; He would give Moses the words he needed when he needed them.

Humility recognizes its shortcomings. It knows it does not know everything, but it also understands that God has given each of us gifts to be used in building God's Kingdom. Those who are truly humble can and will recognize the gifts and talents God has given to them and will use these gifts to glorify God. Likewise, a humble person will not be so arrogant as to tell God what He can or cannot do through us. God knows our weaknesses and often asks us to do something in an area in which we are weak precisely so that others might see His strength manifested through us. Humility is an obedient servant of the Lord, not because it trusts in its own strength but because it trusts in God's.

Paul tells us that all of us have gifts that we have received from God. Since we received these gifts from God, we have no reason to boast in ourselves or in our accomplishments. When we acknowledge God as the source of our talents, it will lead us not into pride but into gratitude.

Problems arise when we give pride a place in our lives. The terrible sin of pride blinds us to the reality of our condition. It causes us to take our eyes off the Lord and to focus them on ourselves. As the proverb tells us, "a haughty spirit precedes stumbling", or as some translations put it, "pride goes before a fall." If you remember the story of the original Fall—the story of Adam and Eve in the garden of Eden—you remember that it was pride that led to their downfall. At first, Eve did not listen to the serpent who was trying to tempt her. But then the serpent told her that if she ate the forbidden fruit, she would be like God Himself. This idea appealed to her. She liked the idea of being a god, and so she ate. What a disastrous decision that turned out to be! Ever since that moment Satan has been successful time and time again causing us to stumble by appealing to our pride and vanity. He gets us thinking so highly of ourselves, and he gets us walking with our noses so high up in the air, that we fail to notice the pit he has dug immediately in front of us. Our pride becomes the cause of our demise. Before we allow this to happen, we need to go back and ask ourselves the question that Paul asked of us: "What do you have that you did not receive?" The answer to this question, when taken seriously, should humble everyone. Yet so often pride blinds us to the real answer to this question, doesn't it?

When we lived in Europe, we often rode the subway. If you have ever ridden a subway, you know that as you wait on the platform for the train to arrive, before you can actually see it coming, you can feel the wind pushing through the tunnel in front of it. When we felt that wind, we knew the train was coming. The wind was a sign of what would follow. In the book of Proverbs, we read that, like the wind before the train, pride comes before a fall. This does not mean that every catastrophe is the result of pride; however, it does mean that if we see pride—especially in our own lives—we can be certain a fall is sure to follow.

Each of us, therefore, needs to engage in a bit of self-examination. We need to ask ourselves: Am I proud? To answer this question we need to look for the symptoms of pride. One of the surest symptoms is the tendency to judge, or to criticize, other people because you cannot easily criticize someone else when you are keenly aware of your own sins and weaknesses. You are unlikely to condemn others when you know that you yourself are a sinner saved by the grace of God. Pride, however, is quick to judge and criticize. It will try to make itself look good by making others look bad. It will criticize, compare, and judge in such a way that it will put others in a bad light and so make itself look good in comparison.

Another symptom of pride is the tendency to be argumentative. The Bible tells us the argumentative spirit is born out of pride and where there is no pride, there is no contention. Do you live, or work, in an environment that always feels rife with contention? If so, examine yourself to see if you are the cause. Examine yourself to see if you are the one being combative. You may well think your spouse is really the source of all the trouble, or you may think your co-workers or colleagues are the ones who are proud. In fact, they may very well be. But you might own a share of the guilt as well. An argument, after all, needs to have at least two parties. One person cannot carry on an argument without at least one sparring partner. Unless at least two people are involved, you simply have a monologue.

Perhaps you have done some reading in modern psychology, which speaks of the importance of self-worth. You may be wondering how a healthy sense of self-worth can coexist with the virtue of humility. The Bible, in fact, does say very wonderful things about us. It says we were made just a little lower than the angels. It says God created us with honor and glory, that He created us in His own image and because of this we are unique in all of creation. It says God has endowed us with wisdom and righteousness and that we are children of the living God and heirs to the Kingdom of Heaven. These are strong statements about the value God has placed on us. Indeed, we are God's handiwork, and we are His children whom He loves beyond what words are able to express. He loves us so much, in fact, that He gave His own son as a sacrifice for our sins.

Nevertheless, we must keep in mind that, along with Adam and Eve, we too have fallen into a state of sin and darkness. A few years ago, I had the pleasure of accompanying a group of my students to Holland to participate in a one-week program. On the next-to-the-last day, we went into Amsterdam to spend the afternoon at the Rijksmuseum, the national museum of fine arts. The place was amazing! It was full of original Rembrandts, Vermeers, as well as works by the other great Dutch masters. Humankind is something like that museum—it is comprised of priceless works of art. But in our case, the museum has been vandalized. The priceless masterpieces have been marred and desecrated. We find ourselves in a very different state from what we once were. The art is still made in the image of the living God; however, since Adam's fall, its original beauty has been distorted and obscured. It has been covered with grafitti, canvases have been slashed, statues have had pieces broken off. We are now an ugly mess. Although we are still children of the King, we have rebelled against our Father. We have brought chaos, destruction, and pain into our lives and into our world. Moreover, we are completely unable to fix the situation or to set things right on our own. We need the help of a Master of Restoration.

Perhaps you read the story of an eighty-two-year-old woman in Borja, Spain, who tried to restore a famous fresco in her church there. The fresco *Ecce Homo* had been painted by Elias García Martínez around 1930. The old woman was bothered by the fact that some of the paint had started to flake, so she decided to take matters into her own hands and fix it herself. Most people found the results of her efforts to be less than satisfactory. How often do we try this self-restoration approach in our own lives? And with what result?

Humility is the first step we must take to get out of our fallen state. Peter tells us that God opposes the proud and gives grace to the humble. No one, therefore, can come to God who is proud. God dwells only with those who have repentant hearts and who are humble in spirit. As long as one is filled with false ideas about being able to restore oneself through one's own righteousness, a person will be deemed less than satisfactory. It is only when we begin to see ourselves as sinners in the sight of God that we can have our sins washed away by the blood of Jesus Christ. We are righteous in God's sight only when He makes us righteous. Our faith must be in Christ and not in ourselves. Our hope is to be found not in our own accomplishments but upon the cross and in the empty tomb. A Christian, therefore, is a person who has ceased trusting in himself and his own accomplishments and who has put his trust in Jesus Christ.

So how do we become humble? We begin by having a proper view of ourselves, our gifts, our abilities, our accomplishments, and by realizing there is nothing we have that we have not received from God. Instead of being proud, we learn to be grateful. And in learning to be grateful, we learn to serve God and to serve one another. Instead of focusing all of our attention on ourselves, we focus our attention on Jesus Christ and the work of His kingdom. We also begin to give frequent thanks to God for all that we are and have.

If we want to be humble, we need to pray. We need to confess our sins to God, and we need to ask Him to remove the sin of pride from our lives that we might become more humble. We need to pray that God will help us mature as His children and continue to change our hearts. Humility is not a show we put on for the benefit of others; it is a realistic appraisal of who we are as we stand before the Lord our Creator. True humility allows us to see everything and everyone clearly, and this clear vision then affects the way we think and act. Whereas false humility draws attention to itself, true humility points people to God. This is what we must learn to do: live in a way that points people to God.

Being humble does not mean becoming a social doormat, allowing people to walk all over us. The apostle Paul, you may remember, was a man of humble soul, aware of his own sins and limitations. At the same time, he was confident in the abilities and gifts God had given him. He knew that he couldn't hide, or squander, these gifts. He claimed to be under compulsion to use all that God had given him to build up the Church, the Body of Christ. Paul had no doubt about the message he was preaching. The message was true, so he never wavered or compromised when it came to the gospel. Although Paul was humble, he proclaimed the good news that Jesus is risen with great boldness. He continually challenged those around him with the truth of the gospel. Humility, therefore, doesn't mean being timid, pretending to be incompetent, or putting on false humility. Humility—true humility—means trusting in the Lord's strength and not in our own. When we trust in the Lord's strength and when we do His work in obedience to His Word, we will find that there is very little we cannot do.

At the beginning of this chapter, I suggested it can be quite difficult to recognize true humility in ourselves and in others. But, in fact, we really shouldn't be looking at ourselves or at others in this critical kind of way to measure how spiritual each of us are. Christianity is not a contest to see who can become the most spiritual. Christianity is not a contest at all! Rather, it is a personal relationship with our Lord and Maker—a relationship based on love. The quest for humility, therefore, neither begins nor ends with judgments or comparisons. It focuses its attention on Christ. Humility is a virtue only attained when we keep our eyes fixed on our Lord and Savior Jesus Christ and when we begin to see ourselves through His eyes.

> Have this attitude in yourselves which was also in Christ Jesus, who, as He already existed in the form of God, did not regard equality with God a thing to be grasped, but emptied Himself by taking the form of a bond-servant and being born in the likeness of men. And being found in appearance as a man, He humbled Himself by becoming obedient to the point of death: death on a cross. For this reason also God highly exalted Him, and bestowed on Him the name which is above every name, so that at the name of Jesus every knee will bow, of those who are in heaven, and on earth and under the earth, and that every tongue will confess that Jesus Christ is Lord, to the glory of God the Father.
>
> —*Philippians 2:5-11*

6

The Body of Christ . . . it's complicated!

Greet one another with a holy kiss.
All the congregations of Christ greet you.

—Romans 16:16

PAUL CONCLUDES THE BOOK of Romans with a lengthy list of greetings:

I recommend to you our sister Phoebe, who is a servant of the church which is at Cenchrea, that you receive her in the Lord in a manner worthy of the saints, and that you help her in whatever matter she may have need of you; for she herself has also been a helper of many, and of myself as well.

Greet Prisca and Aquila, my fellow workers in Christ Jesus, who risked their own necks for my life, to whom not only do I give thanks, but also all the churches of the Gentiles; also *greet* the church that is in their house. Greet Epaenetus, my beloved, who is the first convert to Christ from Asia. Greet Mary, who has worked hard for you. Greet Andronicus and Junia, my kinsfolk and my fellow prisoners, who are outstanding in the view of the apostles, who also were in Christ before me. Greet Ampliatus, my beloved in the Lord. Greet Urbanus, our fellow worker in Christ, and Stachys my beloved. Greet Apelles, the approved in Christ. Greet those who are of the household of Aristobulus. Greet Herodion, my kinsman. Greet those of the household of Narcissus, who are in the Lord. Greet Tryphaena and Tryphosa, workers in the Lord. Greet Persis the beloved, who has worked hard in the Lord. Greet Rufus, a choice man in the Lord, also his mother and mine. Greet Asyncritus, Phlegon, Hermes, Patrobas, Hermas, and the brothers and sisters with them. Greet Philologus and Julia, Nereus and his sister, and Olympas, and all the saints who are with them. Greet one another with a holy kiss. All the churches of Christ greet you.

—Romans 16:1-16

Who was Phoebe? Who were Prisca and Aquila? Who was Andronicus? Ampliatus? Urbanus? Who were all these other people whose names we have a hard time pronouncing? Why does Paul spend so much time mentioning them in his letter to the Romans? After all, this epistle was a serious theological treatise on the doctrine of justification. Why use a whole page of expensive papyrus just to provide this list of names?

Paul made the effort to greet these people because they were his fellow Christians; they were his brothers and sisters in Christ, and they were the building blocks of the early Church. I suspect that when most of us think of the early Church we think first of Paul and Peter and the other apostles, all of whom are most worthy of our remembrance. We often forget, however, that the early Church, like the Church of our day, was comprised mostly of these other, lesser-known believers. The apostles were the leaders. They provided teaching and direction; they kept everyone on track and moving together toward their common goals. They were role models, as well as evangelists and missionaries. We have good evidence that all the original apostles except John died as martyrs because of the witness they bore to the resurrection of Jesus Christ, and John died a prisoner on the island of Patmos because of his faith. We also know the apostles played an essential role in planting new congregations in important urban centers throughout the Roman Empire and beyond. However, they did not establish these congregations or build the Church by themselves. It was the mostly anonymous believers, such as those Paul mentions in Romans 16, who carried on the work the apostles had begun. They were the ones who took the gospel from the urban centers where the apostles had been preaching and brought it out into the neighborhoods and countryside.

Nowadays, when people think of the "Church," they often think of a big, old building where professional Christians wearing funny clothes work. It is a place where individuals go once a week to perform some mysterious, ancient rituals. They believe that if the rituals are done correctly, in accordance with the well-worn traditions, their sins will be forgiven and they will get a shot of grace to help them get through the following week. The problem is, this picture of the Church is completely wrong—and wrong for several reasons. If we read the Bible and pay attention to the details, we will see that the Church is something altogether different.

In 1 Corinthians 3:1-16, Paul tells us the Church is not actually a place where we go. It is not a physical building, but it is a spiritual building, a building in which each individual believer serves as an important brick or stone. Paul tells us that each of us has a unique and special place in this spiritual temple. When we are fitted together according to God's design, we serve as God's dwelling place on earth. God does not dwell within the physical walls of a human-made building; rather, He dwells within us as we are joined together in fellowship. This is consistent with what we read in 1 John 4, that when we love one another, God is present with us and the world is able to see Him in some way through us!

In 1 Corinthians 12, Paul explains this another way. He tells us the Church is actually Christ's Body here on earth and each of us is an individual member of this body:

> For just as the body is one and yet has many parts, and all the parts of the body, though they are many, are one body, so also is Christ. For by one Spirit we were all baptized into one body, whether Jews or Greeks, whether slaves or free, and we were all made to drink of one Spirit.
>
> For the body is not one part, but many. If the foot says, "Because I am not a hand, I am not a part of the body," it is not for this reason any less a part of the body. And if the ear says, "Because I am not an eye, I am not a part of the body," it is not for this reason any less a part of the body. If the whole body were an eye, where would the hearing be? If the whole body were hearing, where would the sense of smell be? But now God has arranged the parts, each one of them in the body, just as He desired. If they were all one part, where would the body be? But now there are many parts, but one body. And the eye cannot say to the hand, "I have no need of you"; or again, the head to the feet, "I have no need of you." On the contrary, it is much truer that the parts of the body which seem to be weaker are necessary; and those parts of the body which we consider less honorable, on these we bestow greater honor, and our less presentable parts become much more presentable, whereas our more presentable parts have no need of it. But God has so composed the body, giving more abundant honor to that part which lacked, so that there may be no division in the body, but that the parts may have the same care for one another. And if one part of the body suffers, all the parts suffer with it; if a part is

honored, all the parts rejoice with it. Now you are Christ's body, and individually parts of it.

—1 Corinthians 12:12-27

In the same way that your body is a complex organism made up of a multitude of unique parts, all of which function in their own way but work together for the good of the whole, so the Church also has a wide array of different members, all of whom have different gifts, but who are intended to work together with a common goal and purpose. Just as the body only has one head, two eyes, one nose, etc., so the Church has some who teach, some who lead, and those who serve in a wide variety of ways. Yet all of the parts of the body need each other, and they must work together if anything significant is to be accomplished.

Paul asks what would happen if the whole body were an eye or an ear? The body, of course, would die. The idea of an individual body part running around on its own sounds like the premise of a bad horror film or of a comedy! When we hear stories of severed arms running around causing mayhem or of disembodied brains taking over the world, we either scream or laugh. But we do not take these stories seriously because we know these individual parts cannot live and function apart from the body as a whole.

Just as we know a single body part cannot live without the rest of the body, we also know the body cannot enjoy full health unless all of its parts are working correctly and in unison. My son once fractured a small bone in his foot while skateboarding. It was just one little bone, and the bone suffered only a small, hairline fracture; nevertheless, my son was partially immobilized for weeks. Every other member of his body was negatively affected by this relatively minor injury to one small, invisible, seemingly insignificant part.

What happens to the body if the nervous system is damaged? If the damage is severe, the whole body can suffer paralysis. What happens in the Church, the Body of Christ, when gossip clogs its nervous system? Or if one member of the Church gets angry at another, or if one member decides to let others do all the work? Or what happens if one member decides he, or she, can be a follower of Christ apart from the Church—that is, apart from the Body? What happens to the individual that has been severed from the body? And what happens to the body that has lost an important member?

I realize that the ancient Romans didn't play football as it is played in modern-day America. If they had, perhaps Paul would have compared the Church to a football team. One of the reasons I enjoy watching football is that teamwork truly counts in the game. Eleven players from each side line up on the field at a time, and these eleven players have to work in concert to accomplish their goals in the face of strong opposition. When a play begins, each player has a specific job. Some players specialize in offense, some in defense. On offense, some protect the quarterback or block for the runner. Others run specific routes and are told to be ready to catch the ball if it comes to them. It is the same on defense. Each player has a specific job. To win a game, all the players on the team must carry out their individual assignments, but they must do so in concert with their teammates. The best teams always overcome the best individual players.

I have heard people get into passionate discussions about who the greatest football player of all time was, and to support their arguments these fans usually refer to an individual player's statistics. But these are silly arguments because no matter how great an individual player is, that person cannot accomplish anything without a good team and good team-work. People will compare individal statistics, but an offensive player will have better statistics if his team has an excellent defense, and vice versa. Individual statistics mean little in the game of football. Something similar could be said of the Church. Individual accomplishments mean nothing, and no one has any cause for boasting.

Unfortunately, many people who identify themselves as Christians do not recognize that as followers of Christ they are members of a team. All too often, these people imagine they can follow Christ on their own apart from the Church. Or perhaps they recognize the need to be a part of a congregation, but they see themselves primarily as spectators—they think it is their job simply to attend the weekly worship service (as often as it is convenient), perform the old rituals, and cheer for the pastor as he attempts to take on the world all by himself. But how can the Church bring the gospel to the world if one person is doing most of the work? How can one person succeed, or just survive, spiritually without the help and support of the rest of the team?

The last thing Jesus said to His followers before He ascended to heaven was "Go, therefore, and make disciples of all the nations, baptizing them in the name of the Father and the Son and the Holy Spirit, teaching them to follow all that I commanded you; and behold, I am with you always, to the end of the age." (Matthew 28:19-20). As followers of Christ, this is our mission. This is what He has told us to do. He wants us to help the people who are living in spiritual darkness find and meet God and then become His disciples. How are we supposed accomplish this? John tells us that the world sees God through us when we love one another. The thing is, love is not simply a theory. It is not like some abstract mathematical formula. It can only be seen when it is put into action, and it cannot be put into action and demonstrated in isolation.

This is too important not to repeat it: *Love cannot be put into action and demonstrated in isolation!* Do you see how important it is for us to stand together? We cannot fulfill the mission our Master has given us if we remain cut off from one another. As followers of Christ, we don't come together to perform old rituals or cheer on the pastor; we come together so the world can see God dwelling within us.

I once read about a church in a small alpine village in Germany that had no internal source of light—no lamps, no chandeliers, no windows. I have forgotten the name of the village, but I remember that the expectation in this community was that each member of the congregation would bring a candle or lamp whenever the people gathered to worship or to pray or to share a meal. When most of the members came and brought some source of light, the hall was brightly lit. The opposite was also true: if too many people stayed away, or if not enough people contributed any light, the congregation produced little heat or illumination.

Some will argue that the reason they do not join a local congregation is that the Church is full of hypocrites. They also claim their faith is a personal matter between themselves and God. Both of these statements have some truth in them. The Christian life does begin with a personal relationship with God. However, if we are in a right relationship with God, we will also recognize that we are part of His Body. This body is not perfect by any means. It is made up of fallen individuals such as you and me. A wise person once told me not to waste my time looking for the perfect congregation, because it does not exist. And even if it did exist, I would just ruin it if I were to join.

Yet John tells us the world gets a glimpse of God when it sees His love in evidence among us. John also tells us God is love and that we were created in His image. His fingerprints are all over us. We need to love and to be loved. However, love cannot happen in isolation. We need each other. God knows the Church is imperfect. I am sure that much of what is done and said in His name causes Him grief. Nevertheless, He has called us to represent Him here on earth. We are His Body. In certain very real ways, we serve as His hands, His feet, and His mouth. When we come together and act like His Body, we learn to love. We learn to love when we choose to put the needs and desires of our brothers and sisters before our own—even when we do not want to. And as we learn to love, we begin to give the world evidence that God is real and that He is love.

Paul may have been the one who initially brought the gospel to many parts of the Roman world, but it was the ordinary Christians mentioned in Romans 16 who, with the help of the Holy Spirit, then shared it with their families and neighbors and carried it out into the suburbs, villages, and countryside. Who were these people? We really don't know much about them. A few are mentioned briefly here and there in Paul's other letters and in the book of Acts. But, in general, they remain anonymous. They were probably ordinary individuals like you and me—people who had ordinary lives, ordinary jobs, ordinary families, but who changed the world by working together as a body.

Paul doesn't tell us much about these believers. Usually the only piece of information he gives is that they were fellow-workers in Christ or that they worked hard for the Lord. If Paul were writing a letter to us today, and if he knew who you were, what do you think he would say when he came to the end of his letter? Do you think he would say, "and greet so-and-so, my fellow worker in Christ?" Or would he urge you to get off the bench and out on to the playing field?

Many people who identify themselves as Christians think it is the pastor's job to carry out the Church's mission, or perhaps they do not even see a need for the Church because 1) the Church is full of hypocrites and 2) they believe faith is a private matter between themselves and God. The New Testament, however, gives us a different picture of how things ought to be.

First of all, the model of the Church we see in the New Testament is one in which the pastor's primary task is to build up the saints (that's us) and equip *them* to bring the gospel into the community. In Ephesians 4:11 Paul tells us that some Christ gave "as apostles, some as prophets, some as evangelists, some as pastors and teachers." Why? Paul goes on to say, "for the equipping of the saints for the work of ministry, for the building up of the body of Christ." As we gather for worship, and as you listen to whoever may be up front preaching from the Word of God, you ought not be doing so merely as a cheerleader. Instead, realize you are a part of the team, that you too must be equipped for the work of service. If you are not actively exercising your talents on behalf of Jesus Christ, you are handicapping the Church in its efforts to fulfill its purpose. You are causing your team to play short-handed.

Compared to what Paul wrote in the first fifteen chapters of Romans, chapter 16 may, at first glance, seem somewhat mundane. It may appear to lack the depth and profundity of his discussion of justification. But when we stop and think about who all these people were and the role each one played in establishing the early Church, suddenly this list of names becomes much more important.

Paul began his letter to the Romans by telling his readers that all of us have sinned and fallen far short of the glory of God. Each of us, whether Jew or Gentile, according to our deeds is deserving of death. Instead of acting selflessly and putting the needs and desires of others before our own, we have chosen to act selfishly—again and again. We have sinned against God, and we have sinned against one another. But God, because of His passionate love for us, provided an atonement for our sins. He provided a bridge by which we might become reconciled with Him. That atonement, that bridge, is Jesus Christ. When Christ allowed Himself to be nailed to the cross, He was offering Himself as a sacrifice for the sins of all those who would accept what He was doing for them. When He rose from the dead on the third day, He broke the power that death had over our souls. He gave new life to all who would put their lives in His hands. So now all who put their trust in Him are justified not by anything that they might do but simply by their faith.

Faith, however, is more than just words. The substance of our faith will always be revealed through our actions. If our faith is real, it will be visible in how we live as we give our lives to the service of God and to the service of one another. What form will this service take? The chief command that our Lord has given us is to make disciples of all the nations, to bring the good news of what Christ has done to those still living in darkness, to those still dead in their sins. Primarily we will accomplish this mission as the complex organism known as Body of Christ. We will accomplish our mission by working together as a body, or as a team, complementing each other with our various gifts and diverse skills while striving toward the same goal. We will do this primarily by displaying the love of God to those around us, through our words and actions, and especially by the way we treat one another.

7

The Body of Christ:
The Communion of Saints

ONE OF THE CENTRAL activities in the life of the Church, since its earliest days, has been the communal celebration of the Lord's Supper. You are probably familiar with what the apostle Paul wrote 1 Corinthians 11:17-34:

> Now in giving this next instruction I do not praise you, because you come together not for the better, but for the worse. For, in the first place, when you come together as a church, I hear that divisions exist among you; and in part I believe it. For there also have to be factions among you, so that those who are approved may become evident among you. Therefore when you come together it is not to eat the Lord's Supper, for when you eat, each one takes his own supper first; and one goes hungry while another gets drunk. What! Do you not have houses in which to eat and drink? Or do you despise the church of God and shame those who have nothing? What am I to say to you? Shall I praise you? In this I do not praise you.
>
> For I received from the Lord that which I also delivered to you, that the Lord Jesus, on the night when He was betrayed, took bread; and when He had given thanks, He broke it and said, "This is My

body, which is for you; do this in remembrance of Me." In the same way He also took the cup after supper, saying, "This cup is the new covenant in My blood; do this, as often as you drink it, in remembrance of Me." For as often as you eat this bread and drink the cup, you proclaim the Lord's death until He comes.

Therefore whoever eats the bread or drinks the cup of the Lord in an unworthy way, shall be guilty of the body and the blood of the Lord. But a person must examine himself, and in so doing he is to eat of the bread and drink of the cup. For the one who eats and drinks, eats and drinks judgment to himself if he does not properly recognize the body. For this reason many among you are weak and sick, and a number are asleep. But if we judged ourselves rightly, we would not be judged. But when we are judged, we are disciplined by the Lord so that we will not be condemned along with the world.

So then, my brothers and sisters, when you come together to eat, wait for one another. If anyone is hungry, have him eat at home, so that you do not come together for judgment. As to the remaining matters, I will give instructions when I come.

The celebration of the Lord's Supper, Communion, or the Eucharist, as those of different theological traditions call it, has always been a central activity in the life of the Church. Our Lord Himself, on the night He was betrayed, commanded His disciples to celebrate this meal from that time forward whenever they would gather together to remember Him. It is one of only two sacraments recognized almost universally by Christians of different denominations. There are few who question the importance of this meal or who would argue against its celebration. Yet many Christians do not really understand its significance or know what it is we are doing when we gather together to share in this meal.

For some, the Lord's Supper is thought to be an act of individual piety. They approach the sacrament as a private transaction between God and the believer. Therefore, when the meal is being served, these Christians tend to draw inward and cut themselves off from the rest of the congregation. They hardly acknowledge the presence of their neighbors, except when they are required to convey the tray of pre-cut bread cubes or the tray of individual plastic cups of grape juice to those sitting next to them in the pew. At that point, they are forced to make contact with their brethren. Otherwise, these believers try to lose themselves in their pious thoughts and pious prayers.

For others, the Lord's Supper is little more than a memorial service, a time simply for remembering Christ's death and resurrection. Since these believers feel they can remember Christ just as well in other ways, they only participate in this meal on sporadic occasions and then only out of a sense of obligation.

For still others, the Lord's Supper is almost magical. They are not really sure what all is happening or what we are doing as we share this meal together. There is an unknown quality about the whole thing. They sense there is something mystical about the bread and the wine, and they are almost afraid to touch or mishandle this food lest they incur the wrath of God.

Since the celebration of the Lord's Supper was meant to play a central role in our worship of God, it is important that we understand just what the Lord's Supper is, what it means, and why we are to celebrate it; and because Paul warns us to "judge the body rightly," we also need to gain a clear understanding of what it means to come together as the "body of Christ."

We can find an account of the Last Supper in each of the four Gospels (Matthew, Mark, Luke, and John). We can also find Paul's teaching about the Lord's Supper in 1 Corinthians 11. When Paul wrote his first letter to the congregation in Corinth, he had to address a number of serious problems that existed there. First of all, factions existed within the Church. As Paul wrote, "I have been informed concerning you, my brothers and sisters, by Chloe's people, that there are quarrels among you. Now I mean this, that each one of you is saying, "I am with Paul," or "I am with Apollos," or "I am with Cephas," or "I am with Christ."" (1:11-12). Paul responded to these divisions by asking, "Has Christ been divided?" (1:13). I wonder what Paul would say to members of the contemporary Church who identify themselves first as followers of Wesley, or Calvin, or Luther, or Meno, etc.? He had to remind the Corinthians that we are all "in Christ Jesus" and if we are going to boast, we should boast in Him rather than in some human tradition in which we take comfort and pride (1:30-31). As he said in 4:1, "This is the way any person is to regard us: as servants of Christ and stewards of the mysteries of God."

Second, Paul had to address those who believed they were in some way superior to others by virtue of their deeper insight into spiritual matters (chapters 2-4). Their pride was leading to divisions in the body. Moreover, Paul had heard that the congregation was tolerating immorality in its midst. This needed to be confronted in a loving manner. Immoral behavior was not to be condoned in the name of Christ. However, some of the Corinthians also needed to repent from their judgmental behavior and their attitude of moral superiority (chapters 5-10). Others needed to understand that all members of the body were necessary. Each person was unique, and each person had an important role to play within the body. No one was more or less important to the healthy functioning of the body because of a particular spiritual gift or talent. All gifts were given by God for the building up of the body as a whole—and not for the self-aggrandizement of the individual (chapters 12-14). It was at this point in his letter that Paul gave his great definition of love (chapter 13).

When Paul wrote this letter to the believers in Corinth, he recognized that the Body of Christ (that is, the Church) was being torn asunder by various factions and quarrels. The Body of Christ was divided. Therefore, when the Corinthians celebrated the Lord's Supper, Paul declared that they made a mockery of the love and unity this meal was meant to symbolize. In fact, their disunity made a mockery of Jesus Himself. Keep in mind the broader context of Paul's instruction in 1 Corinthians 11. Paul discussed the proper celebration of the Lord's Supper as part of his more general teaching on the unity of Christ's Body. When Paul heard that the Christians in Corinth were participating in the Lord's Supper while there were divisions within the body, his words were harsh:

> I do not praise you, because you come together not for the better, but for the worse. For, in the first place, when you come together as a church, I hear that divisions exist among you; and in part I believe it. For there also have to be factions among you, so that those who are approved may become evident among you. Therefore when you come together it is not to eat the Lord's Supper, for when you eat, each one takes his own supper first; and one goes hungry while another gets drunk. What! Do you not have houses in which to eat and drink? Or do you despise the church of God and shame those who have nothing? What am I to say to you? Shall I praise you? In this I do not praise you.

Obvious divisions existed within the Corinthian church. Some people were only looking after themselves at a time when others in the congregation had great needs. Furthermore, various members of the congregation were angling for positions of prominence in the church based on their supposed superiority in matters of wisdom, morality, or spiritual gifts.

Individuals were placing their own wants and ambitions before the unity of the Church—the Body of Christ—and the disunity caused by this behavior was manifest even at the celebration of the Lord's Supper. People were acting selfishly rather than selflessly. Hence, the unity of body and spirit that the Lord's Supper was meant to establish and reflect was absent. In making such a mockery of Christian unity—of the unity of Christ's Body—the congregation in Corinth was making a mockery of what Jesus had accomplished on the cross, for as Paul wrote, "As often as you eat this bread and drink this cup, you proclaim the Lord's death until He comes." So if there was division rather than unity, and if people were coming together to be fed and not to feed, if instead of learning to be servants the people in Corinth were competing for places of prominence and prestige, what was this congregation really proclaiming about what Christ had accomplished through His death and resurrection? What were these people proclaiming to the world when they celebrated the Lord's Supper in this self-centered fashion?

Although it is easy for us in the present to look back and condemn those in the past—especially the Corinthians—we ought to be careful when pointing the accusing finger. Indeed, when we look around us now, we see the Church is no better in our age than it was in Paul's. If we look at ourselves in all honesty, we will have to admit we have frequently come to the Lord's Table with resentment in our hearts toward other members of the Body. Perhaps we have come thinking we were conducting some kind of private transaction between ourselves and the Lord, as if our attitude toward our brethren was of no consequence. If anything, I think we are even more prone to err in our celebration of the Lord's Supper than the Corinthians were because history and culture have done so much to obscure the original intent of this meal.

We do not have an overabundance of source material to let us know what the earliest Christians thought and did. We do, however, have some artwork archeologists have found in tombs and in various homes and places of worship. One of the most common motifs in early Christian art is that of Christ dining with His followers. Sometimes He is shown sharing the *Eucharist* with His disciples (as in the following picture from a second-century mosaic). In other pictures, He is simply seated at a table with a group of followers. The group—the body of believers with Christ in their midst—is shown sharing a meal together in unity around a table. The Lord's Supper was, and is, meant to be a communal activity, with both a vertical component (between the individual believer and Christ) and a horizontal component (between all the believers seated at the table).[1]

---

1. The following picture is a 3rd Century fresco found in the catacomb of Priscilla on the Via Salaria in Rome. It shows members of the Church sharing bread and wine. It is believed to be a picture of an early Christian celebration of the Lord's Supper.

As the Church progressed through the Middle Ages, the Lord's Supper, for a variety of reasons, gradually became a private act, one divorced from any comprehension that the Church was the Body of Christ. By the thirteenth century, the Lord's Supper had become, in essence, a good deed an individual performed in order to procure a certain measure of God's grace. The meal was consumed by the individual, *for* the individual. In fact, one could pay to have others perform this deed on one's behalf (or even on behalf of someone already deceased)!

An understanding of the Church as a complex organic body was lost for a period of time. People no longer viewed the Church as the community of saints called to bear witness to the reality and power of God's love through their love and unity. Rather, the Church came to be seen as a collection of individual Christians all working toward their own personal salvation. The Lord's Supper was no longer a "love feast," a demonstration of how all the diverse members of a complex organism were united in one body through Christ. Instead, it became a deed done only on behalf of an individual sinner, a private transaction between a transgressor and God.

Much of the difficulty in understanding the nature of the Lord's Supper arose from the problem of how to interpret Christ's words, "This is My body." The interpretation that gained acceptance in the ninth century was that the bread and the wine, although retaining the outward appearance of bread and wine, actually become the physical body and blood of Christ. In theological and philosophical terms, the "accidents" remain unchanged, but the "substance" of the elements become Christ's body and blood. This is otherwise known as the doctrine of transubstantiation. Once the doctrine of transubstantiation became the accepted dogma of the Catholic Church, its members were taught that when the priest consecrates the bread and pronounces the words, "This is my body," the bread actually becomes Christ's body. Since we cannot see this transformation occur with our eyes, the priest rings a bell to let us know that the *Host* (derived from the Latin *hostia*, which means *sacrifice*, or *victim*) has been transubstantiated. At that point, it then becomes something to be feared and to be handled with the utmost caution, lest we desecrate our Lord's holy body by accident.

During the Reformation, the Protestant reformers took issue with the doctrine of transubstantiation. Although most of the reformers agreed that Christ, in one way or another, is present when His followers share in this meal, they could not accept that the bread physically becomes His body and the wine becomes His blood. They argued that Christ is present with us spiritually and nourishes us spiritually. The physical elements of the Lord's Supper serve as an analogy to the spiritual reality of this meal. When Christ said, "This is My body," He did not mean literally that "This is My flesh," but "This represents My body and what I have done for you, and what I am continuing to do for you."

Later, various reform movements within the Catholic Church helped it recover some of the corporate understanding of the Eucharist. Nowadays, both Catholic and Protestant theologians generally agree that Christ broke the bread for His followers to show (and later to remind) them that His body was broken on the cross so they might live. Those who receive the broken bread and the wine in faith receive the gift of new life Christ purchased for them through His death. They accept Christ as their head and so become a part of His Body. As part of His Body, they also receive the gift of the Holy Spirit.

Christians from different traditions understand that when we participate in the Lord's Supper, we are nourished spiritually so as to become more like Christ as individual members of the Body of Christ. As John Calvin explained, we feed upon the body and blood of Jesus as we raise our eyes and minds to heaven and are called through the symbols of the Lord's Supper to seek Christ in the glory of His kingdom.[2]

The Lord's Supper, however, in addition to lifting our eyes up to Christ, also ought to turn our attention toward the other members of Christ's Body—to our brothers and sisters with whom we are sharing this meal. The Lord's Supper was not meant to serve simply as an act of individual piety. It was also meant to bind the followers of Christ together in

2. Calvin, *Institutes of the Christian Religion*, 4.17.5, V. 2, pp 1364-1365.

love. The bread we share was meant to communicate the unity of the Body of Christ. St. Augustine, in fact, frequently referred to this meal as "the bond of love." And John Calvin wrote, "For what sharper goad could there be to arouse mutual love among us than when Christ, by giving Himself to us, not only invites us by His own example to pledge and give ourselves to one another, but inasmuch as He makes Himself common to all, also makes all of us one of Him.[3]

The celebration of the Lord's Supper should strengthen not only our vertical relationship with our God but also our horizontal relationships with one another. It is meant to be a communal undertaking and not a private legal transaction. When a body of believers shares this meal together, it should provide the world with a practical manifestation of God's love! The world should be able to see God's fingerprint upon us.

It is for this reason that Paul warns us to examine ourselves so we don't eat the bread and drink the wine in an unworthy manner. He tells us we must judge *the body* rightly before we come to the Lord's table. All too often, Christians take this exhortation as a cue to become overly introspective. They bury their heads in their pews and try to look within themselves for all the sins and hidden faults that might need to be confessed. This is not a bad practice. Indeed, we all ought to be quick to confess our sins to the Lord and to ask for His forgiveness. Nevertheless, this is not all that Paul had in mind when he isssued his warning to the Corinthians.

Remember the context in which 1 Corinthians 11 was written. Paul was not calling for us to draw into ourselves to plumb the depths of our individual souls. Rather, he was calling for an examination of *the body*—the Body of Christ (the Church)—which would lead to reconciliation and unity. If there was any grudge, any misunderstanding, any bad feelings, or any wrong unrighted between one member and another member of Christ's Body, these members were to be reconciled before sharing in this meal.

Paul tells us to judge the body rightly. But what is the body? It is the Body of Christ—the body the Corinthians had been dividing through their selfish behavior. If there is any wound or schism in the Body, it must be healed before we partake of the Lord's Body. Such divisions were present within the Corinthian church, yet the people in the congregation continued to participate in the Lord's Supper. Because of this, Paul told them God was bringing judgment upon them. Because of their uncritical understanding of the Church, Christ's Body here on earth, and because of

3. Calvin, *Institutes of the Christian Religion*, 4.17.34, V. 2, pp 1415-1416.

the divisions they were letting fester within this Body, they were suffering in visible and physical ways. This was a serious matter, and Paul's warning was a serious warning. There are very real consequences when we refuse to forgive one another, when we hold grudges, and when we allow divisions and schism to darken the Church.

We need to realize that when we share in the Lord's Supper we do so as members of the Body of Christ and that together we declare that Jesus offered Himself up as a sacrifice on our behalf. We declare to the world that God loves us so much that His only begotten Son was willing to pay the price for our selfishness. Moreover, the way we celebrate this meal offers testimony to the world about the nature of this divine love. So if we are to celebrate this meal correctly, we must demonstrate to the world what true love looks like in practice. We must show them what "the body" was meant to be.

Christ was broken for us that we might become members of His Body. When we join with other members of our congregation to share this meal, we do so as the Body of Christ sharing in the Body of Christ so we might become more like the Body of Christ. In the future, when we have the opportunity to celebrate this meal together, let us examine ourselves. If any divisions exist among us, if there are any wounds that have not been healed, any hard feelings, or any matters that must be reconciled, we must set aside our pride and resolve these matters before coming to the Lord's Table. Let us, with God's Spirit, celebrate the Good News of Jesus Christ as well as our unity as His Body. Together let us proclaim our Lord's death and his triumphant resurrection.

The Lord's Supper is not something to be feared unless we are harboring ill will toward one or more of our brethren, nor is the Supper magical in any way. It is, however, a mystery—that is, a sacrament. The Lord's Supper is also more than just a memorial service to perform at random intervals. When we celebrate the Lord's Supper, we proclaim our faith in His resurrection. Through our unity as the Body of Christ we also ought to proclaim the reality and power of His transforming love.

> "O Sacrament of Love! O sign of unity! O bond of Charity! He who would have Life finds here indeed a Life to live in and a life to live by."

> —St. Augustine, *Homilies on the Gospel of John*[4]

---

4. St. Augustine, *Homilies on the Gospel of John*, tractate XXVI.13, p. 172.

8

Forgiveness: For the Love of God!

"Then Peter came up and said to Him, "Lord, how many times shall my brother sin against me and I still forgive him? Up to seven times?" Jesus said to him, "I do not say to you, up to seven times, but up to seventy-seven times.

"For this reason the kingdom of heaven is like a king who wanted to settle accounts with his slaves. And when he had begun to settle them, one who owed him ten thousand talents was brought to him. But since he did not have the means to repay, his master commanded that he be sold, along with his wife and children and all that he had, and repayment be made. So the slave fell to the ground and prostrated himself before him, saying, 'Have patience with me and I will repay you everything.' And the master of that slave felt compassion, and he released him and forgave him the debt. But that slave went out and found one of his fellow slaves who owed him a hundred denarii; and he seized him and began to choke him, saying, 'Pay back what you owe!' So his fellow slave fell to the ground and began to plead with him, saying, 'Have patience with me and I will repay you everything.' But he was unwilling, and went and threw him in prison until he would pay back what was owed. So when his fellow slaves saw what had happened, they were deeply grieved and came and reported to their master all that had happened. Then summoning him, his master said to him, 'You wicked slave, I forgave you all that debt because you pleaded with me. Should you not also have had mercy on your fellow slave, in the same way that I had mercy on you?' And his master, moved with anger, handed him over to the torturers until he would repay all that was owed him. My heavenly Father will also do the same to you, if each of you does not forgive his brother from your heart."

—Matthew 18:21-35

"Do not judge, so that you will not be judged. For in the way you judge, you will be judged; and by your standard of measure, it will be measured to you. Why do you look at the speck that is in your brother's eye, but do not notice the log that is in your own eye?"

—Matthew 7:1-3

"And forgive us our debts, as we also have forgiven our debtors."

—Matthew 6:12

IN MATTHEW 18:21-35, JESUS tells us a story about a king who decided to settle accounts with his servants. While examining his ledgers, the king noticed that one of his servants owed him ten thousand talents. I have seen different estimates of what that might be equivalent to nowadays. Suffice it to say, it was a debt well beyond what any normal person, much less a lowly servant, would ever have been able to satisfy. Since it was obvious that the servant would never have the means to repay this massive debt, his lord commanded that he, his wife, and his children be sold into slavery. Moreover, all the debtor's possessions were to be liquidated and whatever money was raised from these sales was to be used to repay some small portion of the total debt.

The servant, however, fell down before the king and begged for mercy: "Have patience with me, and I will repay you everything." The king knew quite well that this man would never be able to repay such a large debt, yet he had mercy. He showed compassion, forgave the servant's debt, and set him free.

But no sooner had this man been spared a lifetime of slavery than he went out and found one of his fellow servants who owed him a hundred denarii. A denari would be about what you could earn in one day at a minimum-wage job. In other words, a hundred denarii was a negligible amount of money compared to ten thousand talents. Nevertheless, the first servant seized the second and began choking him, saying, "Pay back what you owe!" The second servant also begged for mercy, using the very same words the first servant had used when begging for mercy from the king: "Have patience with me, and I will repay you everything." The first servant, however, turned a deaf ear to this plea when it was directed at him. He threw the second servant in prison until the hundred-denari debt could be repaid in full.

When the king's servants heard about this, they became upset and told the king what had happened. The king summoned the unmerciful servant to a second audience, at which he used some rather strong language: "You wicked servant! I forgave your massive debt because you asked for mercy. So why didn't you have mercy on your fellow servant as I had mercy on you?" The king then handed the unmerciful servant over to the torturers until his entire debt was repaid. Jesus ended this story by warning, "My heavenly Father will also do the same to you, if each of you does not forgive your brother from your heart."

Jesus makes it clear that each one of us is like that first servant who owed his lord ten thousand talents. In the context of this story, this was a debt so large the servant had no hope of ever paying it all back. So we need to recognize that we were so deeply indebted to our Lord that we owed Him everything we had and everything we ever would have and we were still without hope of ever settling our account. However, we cried out and begged for mercy. And because we asked for mercy, our Lord forgave us; He released us from our debt and set us free. But no sooner did our Lord forgive our great debt and give us new life than we saw someone who owed us a hundred denarii—a tiny fraction of the debt we had owed our Lord. Compared to the debt we had once incurred, this person's debt to us was nothing! Nevertheless, we assumed the role of judge. We pronounced the other person guilty and demanded justice. We declared that the person must satisfy the debt owed to us.

What happens then? Our Lord calls us back. And when we stand before Him this time, He reminds us that we were also debtors. When we could not repay our debt to Him, He had mercy on us. When we deserved judgment, He forgave us and offered us new life. And what have we done? We have gone out and condemned someone who owed us a hundred denarii. "How dare you!" the king says, "How dare you!" "You say that you want justice?" the King asks. "Very well, then justice you shall have! To prison you shall go until you pay back your entire debt of ten thousand talents. That is justice."

Like the first servant, all of us have sinned against our king and incurred a debt so great we will never be able to work it off. At the same time, others have sinned against us. Perhaps someone you trusted lied to you or let you down in a time of need. Maybe a partner cheated on you.

Perhaps you were wounded by someone in your family. It is possible you were the victim of a crime or you suffered because of someone's recklessness or thoughtless behavior. We live in a broken world, and without doubt you have been wounded. That is part of life on this earth.

The questsion then is not whether you have been hurt; rather, it is how you are going to respond to the hurt. You have a choice. You can forgive the one who hurt you and begin to experience healing, or you can hold on to the pain and carry a grudge. You can let go of your anger, give it to God, and allow Him to be the judge, or you can try pushing God off His throne so you can play judge. In this case, you can continue dwelling on how badly you have been hurt and continue agitating your wound so it does not heal properly. Scripture, however, warns against this second option.

Before we look at what Scripture has to say, let us first consider what it means to forgive someone. Emotional and spiritual wounds are similar in many ways to physical wounds. The deeper and more traumatic the wound, the longer it takes to heal. Some wounds are so deep and so serious that they leave permanent scars. We are commanded to forgive, so we must. Sometimes, however, the hurt is so great that this can only be accomplished with God's help, and even then it takes time and it happens by degrees.

When we forgive someone we do not necessarily forget what that person did. Rather, we let go of our claim to sit in judgment over that person. We let God be the judge. Then we look to the future and do our best to get on with our lives. In some cases, it is easy to forget what happened; in other cases it is nearly impossible.

Imagine you are out shopping one day, when some kindly, old lady you have never seen before accidentally runs her shopping cart over your toe and says, "Sorry!" That deed is relatively easy to forgive and forget. However, if you are betrayed by a person to whom you have given your heart, that will require some time, especially if the other person is not particularly repentant. In that case, I am not sure you can—or even should—forget what that person did. In such instances, forgiveness may simply mean that you give up your claim to sit in judgment over the person and then do your best to move forward, leaving the past behind. If the person is unrepentant, you may not be able to do anything more. On the other hand, if the person does express remorse and actually asks for forgiveness, then you must give the person the opportunity to win back your trust. But trust is not restored automatically. The person needs to rebuild what was destroyed through the unfaithfulness. Forgiveness allows a new opportunity to put things right, but it doesn't pretend that nothing happened.

The Scriptures show us Jesus forgiving. In these biblical examples, the one who is forgiven typically demonstrates regret and remorse, such as when Jesus, after His resurrection, restored Peter, who had denied him three times. These people recognize their sin, and they express a desire to get right with God. Other times, Jesus seemed to turn the unrepentant or unknowing wrongdoer over to His Father, such as when Jesus, while hanging on the cross, looked at the soldiers and the crowd, and prayed, "Father, forgive them." But even when Jesus restored Peter, he said, "If you love me, then do the following."

In Matthew 7:1-5 (which is part of the Sermon on the Mount), Jesus instructed His listeners:

> "Do not judge, so that you will not be judged. For in the way you judge, you will be judged; and by your standard of measure, it will be measured to you. Why do you look at the speck that is in your brother's eye, but do not notice the log that is in your own eye? You hypocrite, first take the log out of your own eye, and then you will see clearly to take the speck out of your brother's eye."

Sometimes we try to convince ourselves it really is okay for us to judge someone else. We rationalize that somehow our case is special and our situation is unique in the history of the world. God just doesn't know how badly we were hurt. But keep in mind that God the Father does know what it is like to lead His chosen people out of slavery only to have them turn their backs on Him and worship idols. He knows what it is like to send messenger after messenger to get His people to return to Him only to have these messengers ignored, beaten, or worse. He knows what it is like to send His very own Son to call His people home and then watch as these people nail His beloved Son to a cross. Jesus knows what it is like to be betrayed by a member of His inner circle—and to be betrayed with a kiss! He knows what it is like to have His closest friends abandon Him in His hour of greatest need. He knows what it is like to be falsely accused, publicly mocked, and beaten for sins He did not commit. He knows what it is like to have nails driven through His hands and feet—nails driven by the force of *our* 10,000-talent debt! Jesus knows what it is like to hang on a cross until His broken body finally relinquishes His spirit. Jesus does know our pain. Keep in mind, too, that even as Jesus hung on the cross, an innocent victim of hate and violence, He still refused to take His Father's place on the throne of judgment. One of the last things Jesus said while on the cross was, "Father, forgive them, for they know not what they do."

Jesus tells us that when we judge another person, God will use the same standard of judgment that we used to judge us. As you judge, so you will be judged. We tend to read these words in the Bible without taking them seriously. We try to comfort ourselves with the notion that God does not really mean what He says. But He does mean what He says. God does not use words frivolously. When He speaks, universes come into existence.

The eyes of our heart should be focused on Jesus Christ and not on ourselves. If we can keep our focus on Jesus, we will see ourselves as we really are—as sinners who have been saved by His mercy. And if we see ourselves as sinners who have been saved by His mercy, we will be much less likely to give pride, anger, and a judgmental attitude room to grow in our hearts.

If you need yet more proof that Jesus meant exactly what He said when He told His followers that they must forgive if they expected to be forgiven, and that they must be merciful, if they hoped to be shown mercy, look again at the Lord's Prayer. You can find this in Matthew 6:9-13. Look in particular at verse 12. Jesus begins by telling us to direct our prayers to our Father in Heaven and to ask Him for forgiveness. I like that part of the prayer! However, Jesus then says when we ask for forgiveness, we are to ask God to "forgive us our debts, as we also have forgiven our debtors." In other words, Jesus told us that we will only be forgiven as we forgive. We will be judged as we judge. That part of the prayer can be a little unsettling if we are not of the mind to forgive.

As followers of Christ, we are not called to judge the world. That is God's responsibility. Instead we are called to lead the world to the foot of the cross. Since we have been forgiven, we are called upon to forgive. Since Jesus humbled Himself for us, we are called upon to humble ourselves for the sake of others. Now that we have experienced mercy, we are called on to show others just where it was that we found mercy. To do this, we must demonstrate mercy through our actions and speech.

A little while ago, I came upon the following photo. It was taken in Alaska by someone who stumbled upon this scene while hiking in the wilderness. In the photo, you can see two bull moose frozen below the surface of a river. The moose were obviously engaged in a struggle. In the course of battle, they had locked antlers, and, it would seem, neither one would back off. So they continued to fight and wrestle until their battle led them into these icy waters. Still neither one would relent; neither would back down. They continued to battle until they both perished, frozen in the river. This picture is a good illustration of what happens to us when we will not forgive. We remain locked in combat, unwilling to back down in our quest for victory at any cost. The other person has done us wrong, and we demand justice (as we see it). But instead of victory, our pride and stubborness only lead to death.

Recent medical studies give credence to the fact that an unforgiving heart leads to an early death. Research synopses published by well-respected institutions such as the Mayo Clinic and Johns Hopkins Medical School show that people who are unforgiving often:

bring anger and bitterness into every other relationship and new experience;

are so focused on past wrongs they can't enjoy the present;

become depressed or anxious;

feel their lives lack meaning or purpose;

lose the sense that they are connected with others and thus experience deep loneliness; and

have a lower life expectancy

On the other hand, the same studies also show that when people let go of grudges and bitterness, they typically experience improved physical and emotional health. Specifically, researchers have observed that forgiveness frequently leads to:

healthier relationships;

improved mental health and higher self-esteem;

less anxiety, stress, and hostility;

lower blood pressure;

fewer symptoms of depression;

a stronger immune system;

improved cardiovascular health; and

a longer life[1]

Are you harboring the seeds of bitterness in your heart? Is there some old wound you are holding on to that you will not let go of? Is there anyone you refuse to forgive? Have you given pride or bitterness shelter in your heart? If so, you need to humble yourself before the Lord and let these things go before they consume you. You need to do whatever you can from your side of whatever divide you may be on to make things right. As Jesus taught in the Sermon on the Mount, "Blessed are the merciful, for they will receive mercy." Be quick to forgive in the same manner you wish to be forgiven.

In 1 Corinthians 13:5, Paul teaches that love does not take into account a wrong suffered. If we claim to be followers of Christ, if we truly love and trust God, we must put this love into practice. This is part of the pattern of God's fingerprint on our lives. This means we must bury our grudges before they bury us. Stop trying to sit on the throne of judgment. Let God be the judge. Be merciful and point others to the One who showed you mercy.

1. For example, see: "Forgiveness: Letting Go of Grudges and Bitterness," November 4, 2017, <https://www.mayoclinic.org/healthy-lifestyle/adult-health/in-depth/forgiveness/art-20047692>; and "Forgiveness: Your Health Depends on It", <https://www.hopkins-medicine.org/health/wellness-and-prevention/forgiveness-your-health-depends-on-it>.

9

Entanglement

Therefore, go and make disciples of all the nations, baptiz-
ing them in the name of the Father and of the Son and of
the Holy Spirit: teaching them to observe all things that I
commanded you: and know that I am with you always,
even to the end of the world.

—Matthew 28:19-20

Since we are surrounded by such a great cloud of witnesses,
let us therefore throw off everything that hinders us and the
sin that so easily entangles, and let us run with perseverance
the race marked out for us.

—Hebrews 12:1

Do not love the world, nor the things in the world. If anyone
loves the world, the love of the Father is not in him. For all
that is in the world, the lust of the flesh, the lust of the eyes
and the boastful pride of life, is not from the Father, but is
from the world. The world is passing away, and also its lusts;
but the one who does the will of God abides forever.

—1 John 2:15-17

IT IS MY HABIT to get up early in the morning to spend some time reading the
Bible and praying before I become entangled in the activities of the day. This
is not a practice that I invented, but it is one I highly recommend. No matter
how busy you think you may be, you will find that your days will go better if
you begin them by spending some quiet time alone with God.

I have also found that if I come to Scripture with open eyes and an
open heart, God has a way of teaching me new things, even from passages

I have read many times before. This happened again just recently. I was working my way through the Gospel of Matthew when I came to Matthew 28:19-20. This familiar text is popularly known as the "Great Commission." Jesus commanded His followers to "Go, therefore, and make disciples of all the nations, baptizing them in the name of the Father and of the Son and of the Holy Spirit." Since these were the very last words Jesus spoke before He ascended into heaven, they carry extra weight. Jesus wanted His followers to remember and put into practice this commandment after He was gone. In essence, He gave the Church its mission statement, or marching orders. Very likely, you have heard these verses quoted with some frequency within the Christian world. Some of us have heard them so often we have become inoculated to them. But as I was reading these verses again not too long ago, one word jumped out at me, a word that often escapes notice when we study this text: *therefore*.

Verse 19 says, "Go, therefore, and make disciples . . . " The word *therefore* is not a meaningless filler word. It indicates that a logical relationship exists between what comes immediately before it and what ensues. It tells us that because the one statement is true, whatever follows does so as a logical consequence. We are meant to understand that verse 19 is the logical consequence of verse 18. So if we really want to comprehend the full measure of verse 19, we must go back and take a look at what verse 18 says: "And Jesus came up and spoke to them saying, 'All authority in heaven and on earth has been given to Me.'" Together the two verses read, "And Jesus came up and spoke to them saying, 'All authority in heaven and on earth has been given to me; go, *therefore*, and make disciples of all the nations . . . '"

The implication is clear. We have been sent out in Jesus's name to make disciples of all the nations *because* all authority in heaven and on earth has been given to Him. As I was pondering the connection between verses 18 and 19, it dawned on me that if we take the coupling of these verses seriously and consider the implications of the logic, we need to ask ourselves some difficult questions. If all authority has been given to Jesus, and if He has commissioned us and sent us out in His name with this authority, why have we not done what He asked us to do? Why have we not fulfilled our commission? What is preventing us from carrying out the task we have been given? Certainly, it is not a lack of authority? So what is it?

The problem, obviously, does not lie with Christ, who commissioned us and sent us out in His name. The problem then must lie with us. The writer of Hebrews recognized this, writing, "Since we also have such a great cloud of witnesses surrounding us, let us rid ourselves of every obstacle and the sin which so easily entangles, and let us run with endurance the race that is set before us." (Hebrews 12:1)

What is it that hinders us, and what is "the sin that so easily entangles"? One hindrance is a lack of faith. If you read Mark 6:1-5, you will notice that Jesus was not able to accomplish much in His home town due to the lack of faith He encountered there. This, however, is a topic for reflection on some other occasion. For now, let's consider "the sin that so easily entangles." What exactly is this sin? What does it look like in practice? How can we recognize it? And how do we go about disentangling ourselves from it so we can run our race with perseverance?

We can find answers to some of these questions in 1 John 2:15-17:

> Do not love the world nor the things in the world. If anyone loves the world, the love of the Father is not in him. For all that is in the world, the lust of the flesh and the lust of the eyes and the boastful pride of life, is not from the Father, but is from the world. The world is passing away, and also its lusts; but the one who does the will of God continues to live forever.

John tells us bluntly not to love the world. That is the real sin and the true root of the problem. John goes on to mention "the lust of the flesh and the lust of the eyes and the boastful pride of life" as symptoms of this sin. I used to skim over this diagnosis of sin and its symptoms and think to myself, "I'm okay. My life is not characterized by these particular lusts." But upon a closer reading of Scripture, I have had to reevaluate my spiritual condition.

If you revisit the account of "The Fall" in the book of Genesis, you will find something very interesting. In particular, look at Genesis 3:1-6. Here, we read:

> Now the serpent was more cunning than any animal of the field which the Lord God had made. And he said to the woman, "Has God really said, 'You shall not eat from any tree of the garden'?" The woman said to the serpent, "From the fruit of the trees of the garden we may eat; but from the fruit of the tree which is in the middle of the garden, God has said, 'You shall not eat from it or touch it, or you will die.'" The serpent said to the woman, "You certainly will not die! For God knows that on the day you eat from it your eyes will be opened, and you will become like God, knowing good and evil." When the woman saw that the tree was good for food, and that it was a delight to the eyes, and that the tree was

desirable to make one wise, she took from its fruit and ate; and she also gave some to her husband with her, and he ate.

Did anything strike you as you read these verses, especially in light of the text from 1 John? If not, look again at verse 6. "When the woman saw that the tree was good for food . . . " This is an example of the lust of the flesh. Nowadays, we tend to associate the "lust of the flesh" with sexual sins—especially with someone else's sins—and so we think we are safe on this particular count. The lust of the flesh certainly includes sexual sins; however, it is much, much broader. The serpent did not tempt Eve with inappropriate sexual behavior; he got her with plain, old food. In fact, he got her with a piece of healthy, organic fruit! She looked at the tree and saw that its fruit was good for food. The lust of the flesh is any kind of physical appetite or desire that controls our behavior. Once this appetite, or desire, has us under its power, it leads us to disobedience.

Our bodies were meant to serve us as we serve the Lord. When our physical desires and appetites—whether for food or for some other form of pleasure—control our behavior, the lust of the flesh leads us into sin and provides evidence that our love of the world is greater than our love of God.

Genesis 3:6 continues and says, "when the woman saw that the tree was good for food, and that it was a delight to the eyes . . . " The fruit was a delight to the eyes! That is the "lust of the eyes." Have you ever seen something that you didn't have, but you wanted and then became preoccupied with how you could lay hold of it? Well, that would be envy, or "the lust of the eyes," another symptom that you love the world more than you love God.

In his letter to the Philippians, the apostle Paul—writing from the discomfort of a Roman prison cell—claimed he had learned the secret of being happy and content in any situation with whatever God had given him. Is that true of you? How often is our happiness determined not by our relationship with God, nor even by the blessings we have received from Him, but rather by what we don't have or by what someone else has and we want? How often is our happiness ruined by envy? Politicians certainly know envy is a powerful motivating factor, and they use it to divide us into voting blocks and get themselves elected. Advertisers are also well aware of the power of envy. The next time you watch television, analyze the ads with a critical eye toward noticing how many commercials are using the "lust of the eye" to motivate you to purchase their product.

When our children were little, we spent one Christmas with my mother-in-law. She had received a generous holiday bonus that year, so she went out and bought everything our kids had put on their wish list and more. She spared no expense. That Christmas morning when our children looked under the tree, they found a veritable mountain of presents, which they proceeded to attack with vigor and delight. As our daughter opened present after present, she grew more and more excited. She had dolls and clothes and ponies and all kinds of pink, shiny things. And she was dancing around and thanking Grandma over and over, and she was saying how this was the best Christmas ever and she was so happy until . . . her brother opened one of his presents and discovered that Grandma had given him a Teenage Mutant Ninja Turtle pizza thrower that shot little pizza-looking disks across the room. This was a totally cool present, and she didn't have it. Her younger brother did. In an instant, her smile disappeared. She stopped dancing, threw herself on the floor and started bawling, saying how it was "no fair" that her brother got a pizza thrower and she didn't. A moment earlier, she didn't even know that such pizza throwers existed. In the twinkling of an eye, her happiness was replaced by bitter envy when her brother got something she didn't have.

My family and I moved to Central Europe back in 1993, and I made my home there for more than two decades. When we first arrived in Central Europe, we found that Hungary was not nearly as affluent as the USA; however, it was better off than Romania, which was just to the east. Many Romanians, therefore, looked at Hungary and thought, "We don't need to be rich. If we just had what the Hungarians have, then we would be happy." The Hungarians, for their part, looked at the people in Western Europe and said to themselves, "We don't need to be rich. We would be happy if we could just reach the standard of living that the people in Western Europe enjoy." Meanwhile, the people in Western Europe looked across the ocean at America and said to themselves, "If only we had as much as the Americans have, then we would be happy." At the same time, Americans would watch TV and think, "If only we had the kind of houses and cars and other stuff we see on TV, then we would be truly happy."

But let's go back to Genesis 3:6, which continues: "When the woman saw that the tree was good for food (lust of the flesh), and that it was a delight to the eyes (lust of the eyes), and that the tree was desirable to make her wise"—or as the serpent had told her, to make her like God—(which would be the boastful pride of life), she took from its fruit and ate."

Who among us is free from the temptation of pride? I know that I am not free from this powerful and pervasive temptation. One time when

I was young, our family went on a vacation with a couple of other families we knew. One evening, the youngsters were all gathered around a table playing some card game. The adults were just sitting around talking. While this was going on, one of the parents happened to notice that one of his children was not abiding by the rules. Rather than exposing the child's sin then and there and humiliating the kid in front of family and friends, this parent tactfully summoned his offspring to a private conference. When the two of them were alone, the parent gave this child a choice: the young card shark could either go back out and confess the misdeed to those who had unknowingly been cheated (that is, humble oneself before others) or suffer physical pain through the administration of a spanking. The child opted to experience physical pain rather than humiliation. I suspect most of us would have chosen the same thing. Pride exerts great control, and most of us would (and do) choose to suffer significant pain—physical and emotional—rather than allow our pride to suffer injury. Blaise Pascal, the mathematician and philosopher, once observed: "Vanity is so firmly anchored in man's heart that a soldier, a camp follower, a cook or a porter will boast and expect admirers, and even philosophers want them; those who write against them want to enjoy the prestige of having written well, those who read them want the prestige of having read them, and perhaps I who write this want the same thing."[1]

When we have not won the expected admirers, when we feel that our pride has been injured or that we have been insulted, treated unfairly, or not been given the credit we feel we are due, how do we respond? Do we respond as Christ did with humility and grace, or do we respond in some other fashion? How many relationships do you know of (or have you yourself been in) that have been destroyed or significantly harmed due to pride?

It's no wonder then that John specifically mentioned "the lust of the flesh, the lust of the eyes and the boastful pride of life." They are symptoms of a love for the world, and we can see examples everywhere we look—even within the Church. I can certainly see evidence of them in my own life. This then is the sin that has entangled us—that has entangled me. We love the world more than we love God. This is what is holding us back and keeping us from being obedient to Christ. This is what is keeping us from fulfilling the "Great Commission."

---

1. Pascal, *Pensées*, XXIV.627 (150) p. 208.

Come, Thou Fount of Every Blessing

Come, thou fount of every blessing, tune my heart to sing thy grace;
Streams of mercy, never ceasing, call for songs of loudest praise.
Teach me some melodious sonnet, sung by flaming tongues above;
Praise the mount! I'm fixed upon it, mount of God's unchanging love.

Here I raise my Ebenezer; hither by Thy help I come;
And I hope, by Thy good pleasure, safely to arrive at home.
Jesus sought me when a stranger, wandering from the fold of God:
He, to rescue me from danger, interposed His precious blood.

O to grace how great a debtor daily I'm constrained to be;
Let that grace now, like a fetter, bind my wandering heart to Thee.
Prone to wander—Lord, I feel it—prone to leave the God I love:
Here's my heart, O take and seal it, seal it for Thy courts above.

—Robert Robertson (1735-1791)

10

"Therefore"—A Small Word
with Big Implications

Now Jesus, full of the Holy Spirit, returned from the Jordan and was led around by the Spirit in the wilderness for forty days, being tempted by the devil. And He ate nothing during those days, and when they had ended, He was hungry. And the devil said to Him, "If You are the Son of God, tell this stone to become bread." And Jesus answered him, "It is written: 'Man shall not live by bread alone.'"

And he led Him up and showed Him all the kingdoms of the world in a moment of time. And the devil said to Him, "I will give You all this domain and its glory, for it has been handed over to me, and I give it to whomever I want. Therefore if You worship before me, it shall all be Yours." Jesus replied to him, "It is written: 'You shall worship the Lord your God and serve Him only.'"

And he brought Him into Jerusalem and had Him stand on the pinnacle of the temple, and said to Him, "If You are the Son of God, throw Yourself down from here; for it is written: 'He will give His angels orders concerning You, to protect You,' and 'On their hands they will lift You up, so that You do not strike Your foot against a stone.'" And Jesus answered and said to him, "It has been stated, 'You shall not put the Lord your God to the test.'"

And so when the devil had finished every temptation, he left Him until an opportune time.

—Luke 4:1-15

OVER THE LAST YEAR or so, I have read several articles and books that have made the sad observation that Christianity, as practiced in the West, has become largely indistinguishable from the world around it. For example, based on research conducted by his organization, George Barna has noted that there is "little discernible difference in the core behaviors and lifestyle attitudes and values of born-again Christians when compared with other Americans."[1] Studies carried out in Scotland and Germany have led researchers to similar conclusions with respect to the populations of those two countries.

We still call ourselves Christians, and we like to think of ourselves as being in some way better than the people around us; however, statistics tell a different story. Sociological research has shown that, for the most part, people who consider themselves to be Christians think and act the same way as the rest of the world. Statistically, people who identify themselves as Christians lie about as often as those who say that they are not Christians. Christians cheat in school and cheat on their taxes about as often as non-Christians. They even cheat in their relationships and get divorced just about as often as non-Christians. We see this same pattern in other areas of our lives, as well. So, instead of serving as light to a world lost in darkness, the Church has acculturated itself to that darkness. We are supposed to serve as salt, but we have lost our special flavor and preservative value. As such, we have become ineffective and irrelevant. Hence, the Great Commission is going unfulfilled.

How did the Church fall into such a sad state? I suspect a careful analysis of the problem will show that the answer is not simple and that it has more than one part. However, when all is said and done, we will find that a major root of the problem is this: we love the world and the stuff that is in the world. As a result, we are controlled by our physical desires and appetites; our happiness is determined not by our relationship with Jesus but by the things we possess—or perhaps more accurately, by the things we do not possess but want to possess; and our pride remains a major motivational force in our lives.

So how do we become light and salt once again? Luke 4:1-12 offers some clues. This is the account of when Satan tempted Jesus in the wilderness. Immediately prior to this, Jesus had been baptized, and He was about to embark on His public ministry. First, however, the Spirit led Him out into the wilderness for a time of prayer, fasting and testing.

Have you ever noticed how the three temptations Jesus faced in the desert mirrored the three temptations Adam and Eve faced in Genesis? When Eve looked at the forbidden fruit, she saw that it was good for food. In Luke 4:3, we read that the devil said to Jesus, "If You are the Son of God, tell this stone to become bread." After forty days of fasting, do you think

1. Barna, *America at the Crossroads*, p. 63.

Jesus might have been a little hungry? Those rocks were probably looking mouth-wateringly delicious at that moment. He was hungry; His body was aching for food. The devil, armed with this knowledge, tempted Jesus with the lust of the flesh: "If You are the Son of God, obey Your appetite and tell this stone to become bread." Jesus, however, refused to allow His physical appetite and desires to gain control over Him. Instead, He responded by saying that He drew His nourishment from the Word of God. This same source of nourishment is available to us!

The devil then tempted Jesus with the lust of the eyes. He showed Jesus all the kingdoms of the world. "Hey, look at all this cool stuff. It's mine, but if You will worship me, I will give it to You. What would You rather have, an easy life and all this stuff I am showing You, or a relationship with Your heavenly Father, which, by the way, is going to require You to be humiliated, beaten, and nailed to a cross?" Jesus chose the relationship with His Father and the deep joy and contentment that came with it, despite the hardships He knew He would face as a result. Where do you find joy and contentment, in having the things of this world or in your relationship with God?

Having been foiled in his first two attempts to trip Jesus up, the devil moved on to the third temptation, the boastful pride of life: "If You really are God, make the angels serve You. Throw Yourself off this pinnacle and make them catch You. Behave in a way that puts You in the spotlight and makes others serve You instead of humbling Yourself and serving them. Make them acknowledge Your greatness. Get the credit that You deserve." Jesus did not fall for that temptation. Unlike Adam and Eve, who were trying to become like God, Jesus—the second Adam—did not see equality with the Father as something to be grasped. He had come to serve rather than to be served. He had not come to judge others, but to be judged and found guilty in our place. He had come to lay down His life so that we might have new life.

How then can we let other people know about this gift of new life? How can we, as God's people, carry out the Great Commission He has given us? How can we become free from the sin that so easily entangles us so we might run with endurance the race set before us? For one thing, we can practice the spiritual disciplines, such as fasting. We must keep in mind, however, that we do not practice these disciplines in order to manipulate God or to appear holier than our neighbors. These disciplines were not meant to boost our spiritual standing with the Almighty nor enhance our status within the community of the religious. The spiritual disciplines are simply tools to help free us from the power the stuff of this world has over us. By themselves, the spiritual disciplines cannot save us, for they only treat the symptoms of our spiritual disease. We need to go deeper to get to the root of the problem.

Some, though, would deny that there actually is a problem within the Church. They would say that the Church is doing just fine. Instead, they would argue that the problem with the world today is the heretics and pagans. It is their errors and their malfeasance causing all of our problems. If only we could force the evildoers and the unorthodox to follow our rules of righteous behavior, we could fix the moral decay in our society and set the nation and the world aright. Those who make this argument believe that the lack of light in the world today is due to the power of the darkness out there in the world. They suppose the problem is external to the Church and external to our hearts. But, in truth, the problem lies within the Church and within our hearts. Any physicist will tell you that darkness cannot overcome light because darkness is simply the absence of light. If you want to disperse the darkness, shine a light!

The reason the Church is not fulfilling the Great Commission has nothing to do with the behavior of the people outside our gates. The people out there are not responsible for the Church losing its flavor and becoming indistinguishable from the world around it. The problem, you see, is within. The problem is me. I have an unfaithful heart, and I am in love with the world.

The good news is that Jesus Christ does not give up on us. Although we are often seduced by the world, Christ stood firm in the face of temptation. Instead of acting out of pride, He humbled Himself. He became a servant and laid down His life as a sacrifice to atone for our sins. Why? Because He loves us with a mad, passionate, burning love, and He wants to spend all eternity with us. And what does He want from us in return? First and foremost, He wants us to put an end to our love affair with the world. He wants us to love Him with an undivided heart and with all of our mind, soul, and strength. Within that love relationship, He will help us become the light we were meant to be.

In the book of II Chronicles, we can read how King Solomon built the great temple as a place where God's people could come and worship Him. When the temple was dedicated, God promised that if His people would love Him with all their hearts and would obey Him, He would remain with them and bless them. However, He also warned that if they turned away from Him and started giving their attention and devotion to the idols of the world, He would discipline His people. He would shut up the heavens so it would not rain and crops would fail. He would send plagues and natural disasters. However, in II Chronicles 7:14, God also says, when this happens, "If My people, those who are called by My name, will humble themselves and pray and seek My face and turn from their wicked ways, then I will hear from heaven and will forgive their sins and will heal their land."

Where does this healing process begin? Where does revival begin? God does not say this will happen when the unbelievers repent. He does not say when the pagans shape up and begin following the rules. He says, "When *My people*—the people who are called by My name—when they humble themselves." It begins with us, with our hearts. It begins when we turn away from the world and give our hearts back to Christ. It begins when we humble ourselves and pray. We must take our boastful pride of life and lay it on the altar as a sacrifice to Christ.

In addition to sacrificing our pride, we need to pray. Prayer just means communicating with God, doesn't it? Effective prayer, like any form of effective communication, is two-way. You need to speak to God and pour out your heart to Him. When you do this, you must do more than simply recite a wish list or repeat the words to someone else's prayer as if they were a magic incantation. You need to praise God, thank Him, and open your heart to Him. Then, after you speak to God, you need to listen to what He says in return.

We need to seek God's face! In II Chronicles 7:14, the verb *to seek* is an active and ongoing verb. Sometimes Protestants criticize Catholics because they say Catholics think they can get into heaven if they are able to check off a list of so-called "good works" they have done. But often Protestants think they can just as easily get into heaven by checking off a list of correctly formulated doctrines they can give their intellectual assent to. But God does not want your dead doctrines any more than He wants your dead works. He wants you! He wants to be in a living, loving relationship with you. And like any living relationship, this is going to require active, ongoing effort.

Have you ever fallen in love? Do you remember the early days of your romance when you first fell in love with your sweetheart? Do you remember the lengths to which you would have gone just to spend time with your first love to get to know that person better? Perhaps you would even have made a fool of yourself to get the attention of the object of your affections. God wants you to seek after Him actively, the same way you would have spent your time, energy, and resources to pursue your first love.

Look at Revelation 3:15-20. Here, Jesus instructed the apostle John to write to the Christians in Laodicea:

> I know your deeds, that you are neither cold nor hot; I would that you were cold or hot. So because you are lukewarm, and neither hot nor cold, I will vomit you out of My mouth. Because you say, "I am rich, and have become wealthy, and have no need of anything," and you do not know that you are wretched, miserable, poor, blind, and naked, I advise you to buy from Me gold refined by fire so that you may become rich, and white garments so that you may clothe yourself and the shame of your nakedness will not be revealed; and eye salve to apply to your eyes so that you may see. Those whom I love, I rebuke and discipline; therefore be zealous and repent. Behold, I stand at the door and knock; if anyone hears My voice and opens the door, I will come in to him and will dine with him and he with Me.

Often, we hear Christians quote this last sentence to people who do not yet know Christ as an invitation to become one of His followers. But John was told to write these words to the church in Laodicea, to people who already considered themselves faithful Christians but whose relationship with Christ had become lukewarm: "Behold, I stand at the door and knock; if anyone hears My voice and opens the door, I will come in to him and will dine with him and he with Me." John ends this passage by writing, "The one who has an ear, let him hear what the Spirit says to the churches." (Revelation 3:22)

Has your relationship with Christ grown lukewarm? Has a love for the things of this world started to take precedence over a love for Christ? Are the symptoms of this love visible in your life? Behold, He stands at the door. Will you invite Him back into your life and give Him your heart once again?

As we look around us, we can see a society gone mad. It is a society that loves the world and the things of this world more than it loves Christ. It is a society that has become a slave to the lust of the flesh, the lust of the eyes, and the boastful pride of life. To a large extent, the people of God, instead of serving as salt and light, have acclimated themselves to the darkness and become part of the problem.

Often we try to lay the responsibility for this mess on someone else's shoulders. We speak about what others need to change and what others need to do differently. Sometimes, we even try to put the responsibility for fixing this world on the shoulders of politicians. If only the right candidate, or the right party, could get elected, they would make laws that would fix things. Or, if only those people who are not me would stop their sinful behavior, then things would be set right. But the problem, my brothers and sisters, is not out there. It is right here. The reason society has gone mad and the Great Commission has not been fulfilled is *us*. We do not love Christ with all of our hearts. We have been unfaithful lovers. We have been having an affair with the world. We are controlled by the lust of the flesh, the lust of the eyes, and the boastful pride of life. But Christ has not given up on us. He stands at the door and knocks. Will you let Him back in?

Look again at the Great Commission (Matthew 28:18-20) and at that word "therefore." If we leave out the word *therefore,* thereby separating verse 19 from verse 18, essentially we are left with a command we must try to fulfill through our own strength. That is something that we simply cannot do! If, however, we remain in a passionate relationship with Christ, keeping that first love alive and setting aside our pride to humble ourselves before Him, then with His authority we can make disciples of the nations (beginning with our own community). Because all authority in heaven and on earth has been given to Jesus, we can *therefore* go and make disciples of all nations.

O for a Thousand Tongues to Sing

O for a thousand tongues to sing my great Redeemer's praise
The glories of my God and King, the triumphs of His grace.

My gracious Master and My God, assist me to proclaim,
To spread through all the earth abroad the honors of thy name.

Jesus, the name that charms our fears, that bids our sorrows cease;
'tis music in the sinner's ears, 'tis life and health and peace.

He breaks the pow'r of cancel'd sin, He sets the pris'ner free;
His blood can make the foulest clean, His blood avail'd for me.

Hear him, ye deaf; His praise, ye dumb, your loosen'd tongues employ;
Ye blind behold your Savior come; and leap ye lame, for joy.

—Charles Wesley (1738)

11

First Love

Hear, Israel! The Lord is our God, the Lord is one! And you shall love the Lord your God with all your heart and with all your soul and all your strength.

—Deuteronomy 6:4-5

"'You shall love the Lord your God with all your heart, and with all your soul, and with all your mind.' This is the great and foremost commandment."

—Matthew 22:37-38

WHEN I WAS GROWING up, there was a television show called "Leave It To Beaver." The main character in this show was a boy named "Beaver" Cleaver. In one episode, he was philosophizing with his best friend and offered the judgment that "The worst thing that could possibly happen to you would be if your pet frog died or if you got kissed by a girl." Perhaps you have similar memories of those halcyon days of your youth when life was less complicated.

As I recall, somewhere between the second and third grades boys and girls generally stopped speaking to one another. Boys blamed this separation of the genders on the fact that girls had "cooties." I don't think anyone knew exactly what cooties were—some people hypothesized that they were some kind of infectious disease, while others speculated that they were tiny insects that lived in people's hair—nevertheless, it seemed to be a fact of nature that all girls eventually got them. Once a girl got cooties, it was imperative that boys kept their distance from her. Boys could never allow themselves physical contact—or any form of communication—with a girl with cooties. So, from about third grade on, girls and boys generally avoided one another. The girls, however, didn't really mind this arrangement—except for those girls with the most extreme cases of cooties—since boys at this age were generally interested in things like frogs, lizards, and sports. Moreover, between the third grade and the eighth grade most boys only bathed and changed their socks twice a year. So the girls were just as glad to keep their distance.

But sometime around the sixth grade, the girls began to recover from their bouts with cooties. By the end of the eighth grade, many of the boys had begun to take note of this miraculous recovery. Not only had the cooties failed to cause much permanent damage, but the girls now even appeared somewhat attractive. Once again it became safe for boys and girls to communicate with one another. It didn't take long until certain people got what is technically known as their first "crush." An outside observer usually has no trouble diagnosing this condition. In most cases, the symptoms are fairly obvious. Boys suddenly start taking showers and wearing clean clothes without being coerced, while girls begin monopolizing the bathroom, spending countless hours in front of the mirror.

The crush also caused a temporary loss of rational faculties. One became totally consumed by this new-found affection, going to extremes just to sit, or stand, in the vicinity of that special person and devising elaborate plans to gain the attention of the object of one's crush, even risking ridicule. As I am sure you know, there is little a person with a crush won't do, or risk, to be noticed by that certain heartthrob. Nobody, of course, ever spoke directly with the object of his, or her, affections, but instead communicated through their best friends. These crushes never lasted too long. It was, after all, difficult to carry on a lasting and meaningful crush when one could not speak directly to the love of one's heart.

As time passed, however, we gradually became more adept at communicating with members of the opposite sex, and the relationships we developed with them began to mature. Many of us have even reached that monumental point in our lives where, having completed the ritual of courtship, we have entered into marriage. Those of you who have reached this critical point, or those of you who have watched close friends as they reached it, think back to when the relationship was still new. You, or your good friend, were undoubtedly a little glassy-eyed; your thoughts seldom strayed from visions of your sweetheart; you exhibited public displays of affection, and you couldn't stand the thought of spending any amount of time away from your love. This initial stage of your relationship was exhilarating and exciting. You were abounding in love for your first love. There was nothing you wouldn't do quickly and gladly for the one you loved. There was no request so great that you wouldn't attempt it and none so trivial you would ignore it. You would do anything to satisfy the desires of your true love. You were possessed with that first love that motivates as nothing else in the world can and which can see little else except the object of its affection.

Most of us had a similar sort of experience when, for the first time, we came to know the infinite love of Jesus Christ. At that time, we were deeply moved by the knowledge of what Christ had endured on our behalf and by the extremes to which God had gone to rescue us from the death our sin and selfishness would have brought upon us. Most of us would have shouted "Amen!" in agreement with those words of wonder penned by Charles Wesley, "Amazing love! How can it be that Thou, my God, shouldst die for me?" We were filled with awe, adoration, and affection for the God incarnate who, by His death and resurrection, set us free forever from the condemnation of our sin. We gladly would have done anything if we knew that it would have pleased Him. Jesus Christ was our first and true love.

For most Christians, however, this time of euphoria, both in our marriage and in our relationship with Christ, passes all too quickly. All too soon the honeymoon comes to an end. For various reasons, we fail to sustain the exhilaration, excitement, and inexpressible joy we experienced during that initial stage of our relationship. We have lost our first love. We have allowed the mundane affairs of this world to creep into our lives and assume a disproportionately large amount of importance. We have become preoccupied with the urgencies of the world at the expense of what should be our first love. In this circus we call the modern world, we have lost our perspective and have forgotten what is truly important.

Now, rather than jumping up eagerly when our spouse asks for our help, we tend to groan, complain, and even ignore such demands on our time and energy. Our glassy-eyed looks of adoration have gradually turned to scowls. Unsolicited compliments have now turned to complaints and criticism. In the worst cases, what was once mutual adoration has degenerated into little more than toleration and coexistence. But why does this happen? Why do we let our first love grow cold?

The book of Genesis tells us how Jacob served Laban for seven years so he could marry Laban's daughter Rachel. After this seven years, however, Laban tricked Jacob and gave him his other daughter, Leah. So, Jacob then worked seven more years for Rachel. In all, Jacob gave fourteen years of his life to win the woman he loved. Yet we are told that to Jacob this time passed by as though it were only a few days. The work he did and the tasks he accomplished seemed trivial. His love for Rachel was so great it made his investment of time and effort seem like nothing in comparison to the prize before him.

The book of Samuel tells about David and the love his followers had for him. Although this was not romantic love, it was a great affection that motivated David's soldiers to accomplish great feats for their king. At one point, when David and his army were fleeing from their adversaries, David quietly voiced a desire to drink water from a certain well—a well which at that time lay in the enemy's hands. Some of his soldiers overheard him mumble this wish. So they snuck out to bring some of this water back to David. Why did they risk so much for such a small thing? They would have given anything to please the king they loved. They wanted to give him the desire of his heart and were willing to give all they had to accomplish it.

In the New Testament, we can read of Paul, who, because of his great love for Christ, traveled the world and suffered imprisonment, torture, and finally death. Because of love, he would have gone anywhere and done anything to please his master—and not because he had to, but because he wanted to. So possessed was he by this love, this first love, that he considered nothing to be of value except life in Jesus Christ. To live was Christ, and to die was gain.

Many Christians are no longer possessed by this same burning passion to serve our Lord. We have allowed the newness, the wonder, and the love we once had when we first came to know Christ grow cold. We have let the affairs of the present world cool our passion for our Savior. What was once a close and exciting relationship with the living God has become a proper and formal friendship—perhaps even a business arrangement. We maintain the friendship from long distance, while close to home we are swept off our feet by mundane concerns that press on us with illusory urgency. The flame of our first love has cooled to a comfortable tepidity, while the focus of our attention is turned elsewhere. The honeymoon is over; and although we have not given serious consideration to divorce, our relationship has become burdensome, and we have started to chafe under the demands we feel the Lord is making on our time, energy, and resources. What was once an adventure has become just a list of burdensome chores.

It is tragic when we let this happen in our marriages, and especially so when we let it happen in our relationship with Jesus Christ. In the book of Revelation, an angel instructs John to send the following message to the church at Ephesus:

> The One who holds the seven stars in His right hand, the One who walks among the seven golden lampstands, says this: 'I know your deeds and your labor and perseverance, and that you cannot tolerate evil people, and you have put those who call themselves apostles to the test, and they are not, and you found them to be false; and you have perseverance and have endured on account of My name, and have not become weary. But I have this against you, that you have left your first love. (Revelation 2:1-4)

Christ has no desire or intention of being a forgotten bridegroom in a tired marriage. He wants your full love and devotion.

The book of Deuteronomy records how Moses stood before the nation of Israel and delivered his final sermon before Joshua finally led God's people into the Promised Land. Here, Moses told the Israelites:

> Now this is the commandment, the statutes and the judgments which the Lord your God has commanded me to teach you, so that you may do them in the land where you are going over to take possession of it, so you, your son, and grandson will fear the Lord your God, to keep all His statutes and His commandments which I command you, all the days of your life, and that your days might be prolonged.
>
> Now Israel, you shall listen and be careful to do them, so that it may go well for you and that you may increase greatly, just as the Lord, the God of your fathers, has promised you, in a land flowing with milk and honey.
>
> Hear, Israel! The Lord is our God, the Lord is one! And you shall love the Lord your God with all your heart and with all your soul and with all your strength. (Deuteronomy 6:1-5)

This commandment stood at the very core of Moses' message: "The Lord is our God, the Lord is one! And you shall love the Lord your God with all your heart and with all your soul and with all your strength."

The same command appears in the New Testament in Matthew 22:34-40:

> But when the Pharisees heard that Jesus had silenced the Sadducees, they gathered together. And one of them, a lawyer, asked

Him a question, testing Him: "Teacher, which is the great commandment in the Law?"

And He said to him, "'You shall love the Lord your God with all your heart, and with all your soul, and with all your mind.' This is the great and foremost commandment. The second is like it, 'You shall love your neighbor as yourself.' Upon these two commandments hang the whole Law and the Prophets."

Jesus declared this is the first and the greatest of all the commandments, and it is the very foundation of all that was written in the Law and all that was written by the prophets. It is, therefore, the key to understanding our faith and understanding the proper relationship between faith and works. As Moses tells us, we are to be wholly devoted to the Lord. We are to love Him with all that we are and all that we have. We are to be consumed by our desire for Him. He is to be our first love and the object of our affection and worship.

When we love our Lord to this degree, no task will seem burdensome, no commandment will seem restrictive. Just as you gladly would have done anything for your sweetheart when you first fell in love, so you will gladly do whatever you can to please Jesus Christ. Christ's yoke will indeed seem light—perhaps even non-existent. When, however, this love is absent, even the slightest requirements of our faith will become tiresome. The easy commandments of the Lord will weigh heavily upon you, and you will serve the Lord more out of duty than out of desire. The freedom we have in Christ will seem like bondage as we try to earn our salvation by meeting certain standards of religious conduct. The joyful exuberance we knew when we first experienced Christ's love and learned of His victory over death will evaporate as we start to feel entrapped and as our hearts long after the beautiful, but illusory, temptations of this fallen world. We will remain faithful to God in form, but our hearts and minds will be turned elsewhere. Externally we will keep the Law, but in spirit the marriage will be dying a slow death.

Satan, who is always looking for ways to destroy our souls and wreck God's Church, will do anything to turn us away from our first love. He will exploit every means within his power to strike us at our weakest point. Certainly, his first goal is to divorce us completely from our Savior; but when that is impossible, he will settle for cooling off our passion to a nauseating tepidity. He will seek to make us as palatable as a bowl of clammy, day-old oatmeal served at room temperature. He will endeavor to make our union with Christ a burden rather than a joy; and he will try to deceive us into thinking we are in bondage, rather than allowing us to celebrate in our freedom. He will try to turn us away from our first love, without which our faith is little more than a set of hollow and burdensome rules.

When we find our heart drifting in another direction, or when we recognize that our love is cooling off, we should recall when we first gave our heart to Christ. We ought to remember the freedom we felt and the joy and the excitement we experienced. The honeymoon doesn't have to be over. This closeness doesn't have to be surrendered without a fight. I am not saying our lives can be free of difficulty and pain. True love never grows without hard work, patience, and even pain and suffering. What I am saying is that our relationship with Jesus Christ can be rekindled and reinvigorated. That first love can be possessed again. We must, however, re-examine our priorities. How do we spend our time and energy? With what do we feed our minds? Where do we spend our resources? We must ask ourselves where should we be focusing our hearts, our minds, our souls, and our strength? Do we really find we are any happier when we listen to Satan's lies and pursue his illusory goals? I think not!

Let us return to our first love. It is only there we will find the boundless joy of Jesus Christ. Once again set aside time to be with Him and to get to know Him. Read His Word and give yourself to His service. Love the Lord with all your heart, all your soul, and all your might for there is no other source of everlasting joy. The happiness we seek cannot be found in the things of this world but only in an unswerving devotion to the living God. Make Him the object of your devotion and worship Him with all that you are and have. All that you do, do for the glory of God. Don't let your worship of the Lord be confined to an hour or two a week. Don't let the adventure of knowing the Creator of the universe—the one who spoke the Helix Nebula into existence—become just another routine task. Rather, worship Him continually with your thoughts, your words, and the manner in which you live your life. As Moses once urged the people of God, worship the Lord with all your heart, all your soul, and all your strength.

And Can It Be?

And can it be that I should gain
An interest in the Savior's blood?
Died He for me, who caused His pain—
For me, who Him to death pursued?
Amazing love! How can it be,
That Thou, my God, shouldst die for me?
Amazing love! How can it be,
That Thou, my God, shouldst die for me?

'Tis mystery all: th'Immortal dies:
Who can explore His strange design?
In vain the firstborn seraph tries
To sound the depths of love divine.
'Tis mercy all! Let earth adore,
Let angel minds inquire no more.
'Tis mercy all! Let earth adore;
Let angel minds inquire no more.

He left His Father's throne above
So free, so infinite His grace—
Emptied Himself of all but love,
And bled for Adam's helpless race:
'Tis mercy all, immense and free,
For O my God, it found out me!
'Tis mercy all, immense and free,
For O my God, it found out me!

Long my imprisoned spirit lay,
Fast bound in sin and nature's night;
Thine eye diffused a quickening ray—
I woke, the dungeon flamed with light;
My chains fell off, my heart was free,
I rose, went forth, and followed Thee.
My chains fell off, my heart was free,
I rose, went forth, and followed Thee.

No condemnation now I dread;
Jesus, and all in Him, is mine;
Alive in Him, my living head,
And clothed in righteousness divine,
Bold I approach th'eternal throne,
And claim the crown, through Christ my own.
Bold I approach th'eternal throne,
And claim the crown, through Christ my own.

—Charles Wesley (1738)

12

Do You Love Me More than These?

THE BIBLE TELLS US about two different occasions when Peter went out fishing all night with no success only to have the Lord come along and tell him to put his net down again. Both times, Peter reluctantly obeyed and ended up with a net full to the point of bursting. The first instance is described in Luke 5:1-11. This took place early on in Jesus' ministry. The second occasion took place after Jesus had been crucified and resurrected. We can read about this in John 21:1-17:

> After these things, Jesus revealed Himself again to the disciples at the Sea of Tiberias, and He revealed Himself in this way. Simon Peter, Thomas called Didymus, Nathanael of Cana in Galilee, the sons of Zebedee, and two others of His disciples were together. Simon Peter said to them, "I am going fishing." They said to him, "We are also coming with you." They went out and got into the boat; and that night they caught nothing.
>
> But when the day was now breaking, Jesus stood on the beach; yet the disciples did not know that it was Him. So Jesus said to them, "Children, you do not have any fish to eat, do you?" They answered Him, "No." And He said to them, "Cast the net on the right-hand side of the boat, and you will find the fish." So they cast it, and then they were not able to haul it in because of the great quantity of fish. Therefore that disciple whom Jesus loved said to Peter, "It is the Lord!" So when Simon Peter heard that it was the Lord, he put on his outer garment (for he was stripped for work) and threw himself into the sea. But the other disciples came in the little boat, for they were not far from the land, but about two hundred cubits away, dragging the net full of fish.
>
> So when they got out on the land, they saw a charcoal fire already made and fish placed on it, and bread. Jesus said to them, "Bring some of the fish which you have now caught." So Simon

Peter went up and hauled the net to land, full of large fish—a hundred and fifty-three; and although there were so many, the net was not torn.

Jesus said to them, "Come and have breakfast." None of the disciples ventured to inquire of Him, "Who are You?" knowing that it was the Lord. Jesus came and took the bread and gave it to them, and the fish likewise. This was now the third time that Jesus revealed Himself to the disciples, after He was raised from the dead.

Now when they had finished breakfast, Jesus said to Simon Peter, "Simon, son of John, do you love (*ágapeo*) Me more than these?" He said to Him, "Yes, Lord; You know that I love (*phileo*) You." He said to him, "Tend My lambs." He said to him again, a second time, "Simon, son of John, do you love (*ágapeo*) Me?" He said to Him, "Yes, Lord; You know that I love (*phileo*) You." He said to him, "Shepherd My sheep." He said to him the third time, "Simon, son of John, do you love (*phileo*) Me?" Peter was hurt because He said to him the third time, "Do you love (*phileo*) Me?" And he said to Him, "Lord, You know all things; You know that I love (*phileo*) You." Jesus said to him, "Tend My sheep."

When the Lord appeared on this occasion, He did so with His resurrected body, so Peter and the other disciples didn't recognize Him at first. However, when the disciples followed Jesus' instructions and suddenly found their nets filled to overflowing, John recognized something familiar about the whole scenario. He said to Peter, "It's the Lord!" When Peter heard this, he jumped into the water and swam to shore. There he found that Jesus already had a fire going with some fish and bread grilling on it. Jesus told Peter to add a few of the fish he had just caught to the grill, and He invited Peter and the other disciples to have breakfast with Him.

When they finished eating, Jesus asked Peter, "Simon, son of John, do you truly love Me more than these?" In most English translations this question could be read in one of two ways. Jesus could be asking, "Do you love me more than these other guys love Me?' Or He could be asking, "Do you love Me more than you love these other things in your life?" Fortunately, the original Greek clears up this ambiguity. There we find that the pronoun for *these* is in the accusative form. That means it is the object of the verb *love*. In other words, Jesus is asking Peter, "Do you truly love Me more than you love these other things?" Of course, now the question is what are these other things in Peter's life competing for his affection and devotion? If we look at a couple of other events earlier in Peter's life, we can venture an educated guess as to what "these" other things may have been.

When Simon Peter met Jesus for the very first time (John 1:35-42), Jesus had just been baptized by John the Baptist, and He was about to begin His public ministry. He had not yet performed His first miracle, turning water into wine at the wedding in Cana.

> The next day, John the Baptist was standing with two of his disciples, and he looked at Jesus as He walked, and said, "Behold, the Lamb of God!" And the two disciples heard him speak, and they followed Jesus. And Jesus turned and saw them following, and said to them, "What are you seeking?" They said to Him, "Rabbi (which translated means Teacher), where are You staying?" He said to them, "Come, and you will see." So they came and saw where He was staying, and they stayed with Him that day; it was about the tenth hour. One of the two who heard John speak, and followed Him, was Andrew, Simon Peter's brother. He first found his own brother Simon and said to him, "We have found the Messiah" (which translated means Christ). He brought him to Jesus. Jesus looked at him and said, "You are Simon the son of John; you shall be called Cephas" (which is translated Peter).

When we read this text, we often assume that from this point on Simon Peter followed Jesus around on a full-time basis. But I don't think that was initially the case.

Luke 5:1-11 records events that took place sometime after the events we just read about in John 1. By this time, Jesus had started His public ministry. Crowds were now following Him around, and He was teaching and healing them. Luke 4 tells how Jesus healed Peter's mother-in-law, and how later Jesus sought out a lonely place, perhaps in order to pray and get rest, but the crowds sought Him out and continued to follow Him.

> Now it happened that while the crowd was pressing around Him and listening to the word of God, He was standing by the lake of Gennesaret; and He saw two boats lying at the edge of the lake; but the fishermen had gotten out of them and were washing their nets. And He got into one of the boats, which was Simon's and asked him to put out a little distance from the land. And He sat down and continued teaching the crowds from the boat. Now when He had finished speaking, He said to Simon, "Put out into the deep water and let down your nets for a catch." Simon responded and said, "Master, we worked hard all night and caught nothing, but I will do as you say and let down the nets." And when they had done

this, they caught a great quantity of fish, and their nets began to tear; so they signaled to their partners in the other boat to come and help them. And they came and filled both of the boats, to the point that they were sinking. But when Simon Peter saw this, he fell down at Jesus' knees, saying, "Go away from me, Lord, for I am a sinful man!" For amazement had seized him and all his companions because of the catch of fish which they had taken; and likewise also James and John, sons of Zebedee, who were partners with Simon. And Jesus said to Simon, "Do not fear; from now on you will be catching people." When they had brought their boats to land, they left everything and followed Him.

So in John 1 we can read that Simon met Jesus for the first time when Andrew told him that Jesus was the Messiah. Some kind of relationship was established with Jesus at that point. We know, for example, that Jesus gave Simon a new name, *Cephas*, or *Peter*. In Luke 4, we can read that Jesus healed Simon's mother-in-law. And in Luke 5, we see that Peter referred to Jesus as "Master". Yet while Jesus was teaching and healing more or less on a full-time basis, Peter was still working as a fisherman, at least some of the time. Here we read that while Jesus had been ministering to the crowd, Peter had been out working with his business partners James and John. Perhaps at this time in his life Peter was spending time with Jesus when his work schedule allowed, but clearly he had not yet left everything behind to follow the Lord. That didn't happen until this encounter at Lake Gennesaret (Luke 5:11).

There are probably several reasons why Peter was a part-time disciple. For one thing, you have to be careful about who you go following around. How much did Peter really know about this Jesus guy? I am sure he was thankful Jesus had healed his mother-in-law. Nevertheless, Peter had a family and a business to think about. He had bills to pay. He had responsibilities. Moreover, he knew how to catch fish. He was good at it. This was something safe and predictable. Leaving everything behind to follow Jesus might not be safe, and certainly it was not predictable. If Peter were to give up everything to follow the Lord, he would lose whatever control he thought he had over the direction of his life.

This Jesus fellow probably seemed remarkable in many ways. Undoubtedly, Peter was hopeful that the whole Messiah thing would work out and the Romans would be driven out of Israel. But let's face it, it is a bit risky getting involved with radicals like Jesus, especially if you are going to leave everything behind in the process. So maybe Peter figured he could watch from the sidelines for a while without fully committing himself. Peter probably decided to play it safe and stick with fishing until he could learn more about Jesus and see where He was going. He was probably listening to Jesus when his schedule allowed, perhaps for an hour or two on Sunday mornings, but he was still spending most of his time doing what he had always done, fishing. But when Jesus performed this miracle on Lake Gennesaret, Peter knew beyond a shadow of a doubt that Jesus was the Lord. And when Peter found himself in the presence of the Messiah, he recognized his own unworthiness. In Luke 5:8, we read that "when Simon Peter saw this, he fell down at Jesus' knees, saying 'Go away from me, Lord, for I am a sinful man!'" But the Lord, with a firm tenderness, told Peter He wanted him to become a fisher of people. That is when Peter left everything to follow Jesus.

The shared breakfast on the beach comes later, after Jesus had been crucified. Reports of the resurrection were circulating. The women who had gone to Jesus' tomb claimed they had seen Him. So, too, had the men on the road to Emmaus. In John 20:19-29, we can read that Jesus had appeared to the disciples, including Peter, on two different occasions. But where do we find Peter in John 21? Back at his old, familiar job. He was fishing, doing what was safe and comfortable.

Maybe Peter still felt guilty because he had denied Jesus three times the night the Lord had been arrested. Maybe he felt he was no longer worthy of being numbered among the disciples of Jesus. Maybe he thought he had to atone for his sin and do something in order to earn back God's love. It could be he thought his sin was too great to be forgiven, for he had denied his Lord. It is interesting to note that Jesus asked Peter three times whether Peter really loved Him.[1] It is almost as if the Lord was giving Peter a chance to recant those three denials.

Or maybe Peter just didn't know yet what to make of the resurrection. Maybe he was still having a hard time believing what he had heard and seen. So he went back to something he did understand—catching fish.

Maybe Peter was afraid. On the night Jesus was arrested, Peter had not shown himself to be a "Profile in Courage." He had seen what the authorities had done to his master. Maybe he just didn't have the courage

---

1. It is also very interesting to note that the first two times Jesus asked this question, He used the Greek verb "*agapeo*", which is a general selfless love (similar to the Latin *caritas*), but Peter answered with the verb "*phileo*" which is the type of love that binds friends together. When Jesus asked the question for the third time, like Peter, he used the verb "*phileo*". This use of different Greek words for love is worthy of a separate study . . . but that is for another time.

to follow that path. After all, this is not what he had been expecting from the Messiah. He thought the Messiah was going to drive the Romans out and restore the throne of David. But the Romans were still very much in charge. So perhaps he went back to doing something safe that wouldn't cause any offense or draw unwanted attention to himself. Maybe he thought he could follow Jesus anonymously from a safe distance where nobody would know that he was a follower of Jesus.

Perhaps Peter was worried about his financial situation, about providing for his family. Maybe he worried that since he had just spent three years following Jesus around, he had not been able to save enough in his 401k account to retire at a certain age, especially if Jesus was not going to stick around and restore the Kingdom of Israel.

Whether it was out of guilt, doubt, fear, or financial insecurity, Peter went back to what was familiar; he went back to where he was comfortable. Although there was clear evidence that Jesus had been resurrected and was alive and well, Peter went fishing. So Jesus came and found Peter. After the disciples had made their amazing catch and had eaten breakfast, Jesus turned to Peter and asked, "Simon, son of John, do you truly love Me more than you love these?" So what are "these"?

Peter went back to fishing after meeting Jesus for the first time—until Jesus came and called him to be a fisher of people. Then Peter went back to fishing after Jesus was crucified and resurrected—where Jesus found him and gently called him back into service.

Maybe as everyone was finishing up breakfast, Jesus pointed to the grilled fish still roasting over the fire and asked Peter, "Do you love Me more than you love these fish? Do you love Me enough to leave your boat and your net and come and serve Me with all of your heart, mind, soul, and strength?"

Peter responded, "Lord, You know I love You." But the thing about love is that it is not something theoretical. It is not just an abstract concept. It is something only proven through action. So Jesus went on, "then tend My lambs." Jesus asked him a second time and then a third, responding to Peter's "Yes" with instruction to "shepherd My sheep" and "tend My sheep."

Peter had to break out of the pattern of going back to what was familiar. Whenever he was faced with doubts and uncertainty, he went back to his boat and to fishing. Each time he did that, Jesus came looking for him. With great tenderness and grace, He called Peter to something greater, saying, in effect, "If you love Me more than you love these fish, then I want you to help build My Kingdom. I want you to leave this old life behind to be a fisher of people. I want you to tend My lambs and feed My sheep—to do something risky that requires faith but also something that has eternal significance. We know what Peter ultimately chose, don't we? Years later he would die a martyr's death in Rome, bearing witness to the resurrected Lord.

What are the things that compete with Jesus for your love and devotion? If Jesus asked you, "Do you truly love Me more than you love these things?" what would the "these things" in your life be? And how would you answer that question? What is preventing you from serving the Lord with your whole heart? Is it fear (what will the Romans do?), or guilt or shame (I am not worthy because of sins I have committed), or a certain sense of comfort with where you are in life (I am good at what I am doing, and I know how to do this. I have been working all my life for the financial security of my family and to prepare for retirement)? If you were sitting around a fire with Jesus, and He turned, looked you in the eye, and asked, "Do you truly love Me more than you love these other things"? Would you be able to say, "Lord, you know I love you"? Or would you hesitate? Or would you say "Yes", but qualify it in some way?

If, like Simon Peter, you could look into Jesus' eyes and say with all honestly, "Lord, You know I love You," then Jesus has something to say to you. Love is not some ethereal idea. Love is not empty words; it must be proven through action. Jesus would say to you, "Come and help build My Kingdom. Tend My lambs and feed My sheep."

13

Love and Pain

*Beloved, let us love one another, for love is of God; and every-
one who loves is born of God and knows God. The one who
does not love does not know God, because God is love.*

—1 John 4:7-8

In 1993, my first wife, Diane, and I moved to Central Europe along with
our two children. Despite the initial challenges, we grew to love it there. We
loved the culture, the food, and especially the people. The friendships we
made there will last forever, and it was difficult to leave so many wonderful people behind. However, in February 2014 Diane was diagnosed with
stage-4 metastatic breast cancer. She underwent chemotherapy and radia-
tion therapy there in Budapest, but then we moved back to the U.S. during
the summer of 2015 to be closer to family. We settled in Nashville, where
our daughter and her family lived. Diane fought valiantly and lived her life
to the fullest, but eventually the disease won its campaign of attrition. She
took her last breath on this earth on March 28, 2016.

While we were in Central Europe, I taught English at a public secondary school, and I loved this job. I got to know many of my students quite
well, and we enjoyed discussing a wide range of issues together. During our
last spring in Europe, as my seniors were about to graduate, I had a chance
to talk to them about my faith. As part of this discussion, I told them how
much God loved each and every one of them, and I pointed them to 1 John
4:7-19 where we can read more than once that *God is love*:

> Beloved, let us love one another; for love is from God, and every-
> one who loves has been born of God and knows God. The one who
> does not love does not know God, because *God is love*. By this the
> love of God was revealed in us, that God has sent His only Son

into the world so that we may live through Him. In this is love, not that we loved God, but that He loved us and sent His Son to be the propitiation for our sins. Beloved, if God so loved us, we also ought to love one another. No one has ever seen God; if we love one another, God remains in us, and His love is perfected in us. By this we know that we remain in Him and He in us, because He has given to us of His Spirit. We have seen and testify that the Father has sent the Son to be the Savior of the world.

Whoever confesses that Jesus is the Son of God, God remains in him, and he in God. We have come to know and have believed the love which God has for us. *God is love*, and the one who remains in love remains in God, and God remains in him. By this, love is perfected with us, so that we may have confidence in the Day of Judgment; because as He is, we also are in this world. There is no fear in love, but perfect love drives out fear, because fear involves punishment, and the one who fears is not perfected in love. We love, because He first loved us.

When I finished my summary of this text, one of my very bright students asked a tough question. He wanted to know why, if God existed and if God is love (as I had just claimed) and if God really loved us, then why did my wife have cancer? The fellow was not trying to be a wise guy. It was a serious question. He thought much of what I had said made sense, but he was trying to reconcile what I was saying about God's love with the pain and suffering he could see all around him.

The short answer I gave to this question was that there is pain and suffering in this world precisely because *God is love*. I realize that this may, at first, sound either crazy or cliché, but let me try to explain this paradox.

To make sense of this, we need to consider two important aspects of love. First, we need to remember the apostle Paul's definition of love in 1 Corinthians 13. That passage describes true love as selfless. True love is choosing to put someone else's wants and needs before your own. It is choosing to serve another. Second, true love must be given freely. The obedience of a puppet is not really love, is it? A puppet cannot love, for true love can only come from a heart that is free to put the wants and needs of another before its own.

John tells us God Himself is love. Love is His nature, and He is the source of all true love. We can also read in the book of Genesis that God created us in His image. When God fashioned us out of clay, He put His fingerprint upon us. He created us to love and to be loved. That is the reason we exist. Let's consider for a moment some of the implications of this.

Some people seem to think that in the beginning God first established a list of rules. Once He had come up with these great rules and declared that they were "good", He then created Adam and Eve so that there would be someone around to obey them. But God did not create us just to keep His law. Rather, He created us to love and to be loved. God created us to be His children, so He could love us and we could love Him. God loves us with a love beyond our comprehension, and the one thing He wants more than anything else from us is that we love Him in return. He wants our "first love."

God could have created a world in which there was no possibilty for us to sin and in which there would then be no pain, no suffering, and no death. He could have created a world in which Diane did not have to battle cancer until her body could no longer carry on the fight. But God is love, and God created us in His own image so we, too, might love and be loved. However, in order for our love to be genuine, in order for it to mean anything, God had to give us our freedom. He had to give us the freedom to choose to love Him first and foremost or to choose to love the world. He had to give us the freedom to choose between living selflessly or serving ourselves. Without this freedom, we would not really be able to love. We would simply be puppets.

If our freedom was to be true freedom and not just a charade, then real consequences had to follow from our words and actions. So when Adam and Eve disobeyed God in the Garden of Eden, their actions had real consequences. Death entered our world, and all of creation was thrown into disarray. In his letter to the Romans, Paul says all of creation now groans as it waits for Christ to return and restore it to what it was meant to be.

I have a very wonderful daughter. She is grown up and married now. She and her husband have three wonderful children, and they were a tremendous help to us when Diane was battling her illness. When my daughter was about three years old, Abby loved to watch her mom work in the kitchen, and she was very curious to know what wonderful things transpired up on the top of the stove. She knew Mom was doing something mysterious up there because when Diane stood in front of the stove Abby could see her upper-body movements as she worked her magic up there. Very often, Diane took delicious pots of steaming food from the stovetop and transported them to the table for us to eat. Abby was very curious; however, she was not tall enough to get a clear view of what exactly was happening up there in that mysterious place. So sometimes she would try putting her hand up there to feel around. The problem was we had an electric stove, and it took time for the heating coils to cool down after we had used them. Therefore, we told Abby that she was not allowed to put her hands up there.

Why did we make this rule? Was it to rob our daughter of her freedom and to take away all the pleasure and joy in her life? No, we made the rule because we loved her very much, and we did not want her to get hurt. At the same time, we wanted her to grow up to become a normal, well-adjusted adult. So we never gave serious consideration to keeping her locked up or making her wear a straightjacket so as to avoid any unnecessary rule-breaking. In general, we let her roam about the house rather freely.

Abby, however, seemed to think we were trying to hide something wonderful from her. So one day she toddled into the kitchen when she didn't think anyone was looking. I happened to catch a glimpse of her out of the corner of my eye, so I followed after her. I got there just in time to see her extending her hand upward toward the stovetop. I called to Abby and told her not to put her hand up there. She looked me straight in the eye while reaching up and placing her hand on the side of a hot teakettle—and she burned her hand. She immediately started howling. Then she gave me an accusing look, as if somehow her pain was all my fault.

Often we do the very same thing with God. God tries to protect us. He gives us rules for our own good, but He also gives us a degree of freedom so we might grow in faith and maturity and so we can love freely. But we disobey Him, suffer the painful consequences of that disobedience, and then try to blame Him for our suffering.

There is yet another aspect to the freedom God has given us. As I just mentioned, often we suffer the consequences of our own choices and actions. But perhaps just as often we suffer the consequences of the choices and actions of others. If I choose to shake my fist at God, then I am the one who will bear the consequences of my deeds. However, if I choose to put my fist into your face, then you will also experience pain as a result of my sin.

If love is genuine, it must be freely given. And in order for love to be freely given, we must be free to love—that is, we must have the freedom to act selflessly or to act selfishly. If we are in fact free, then our choices and actions must have real consequences. So it is very possible that you may be the victim of someone else's sin. Likewise, someone else may be the victim of your sin! We don't know the cause of Diane's cancer. Certainly one possibility is human contamination of our environment and our food chain. It is possible that she had to bear the consequences of someone else's actions; we just don't know. However, the Bible tells us that all of us have sinned and have fallen far short of the glory of God. That much we do know.

Perhaps you have had the pleasant experience of being on a beach or a lakeshore on a calm, still morning when the water is smooth and pure as glass. And maybe you have had the pleasure of throwing a rock into the water and then watching the splash generate a ripple pattern of concentric circles spreading ever outward. Sometimes the waves in such patterns can travel quite a distance, disrupting floating objects or debris along the shore. Each time one of us sins, we cause a ripple pattern of sorts. Our words and actions set in motion waves that affect the world around us. Now take the ripple pattern from this one sin and multiply— or amplify—it by the billions and billions of selfish, sinful acts committed on this earth each and every day by members of the human race. The result is a continual series of powerful, destructive tidal waves of sin. That is the world in which we live—a fallen world, stained and distorted by our sin. It is a broken world in which there is great pain. We can see the clear evidence of this all around us.

There are TV evangelists and other preachers who will tell you that if you become a Christian and have faith, God will make your life easy. If your life is not easy, they say it must be your fault. You must lack faith. But God never promises a life free from hardship and pain. The only way He could keep such a promise would be by taking away our freedom. And if He took away our freedom, He would take away our ability to love. He would turn us into puppets, but that is not what He wants. His desire is for children, not automatons.

So instead of putting us all in straightjackets and locking us in our rooms so we can't wreak havoc and destruction, God chose to enter our world, to walk alongside us, and to endure our anguish and misery with us. Jesus Christ came to earth and became one of us. He took on our flesh and became fully human. He knows what it is like to endure temptation, humiliation, scourging, and finally a brutal and violent death on the cross. In the end, He offered His life as a sacrifice for our sins to free us from the power of death. Why would the maker and creator of the universe do this for us? Why would He put our needs and wants before His own? Simply because, as John tells us, God is love, and He loves us with a love beyond the power of human words to describe. He loves us with a mad, crazy, passionate love, and He wants to spend all eternity with us.

In Deuteronomy 31:6 and again in Hebrews 13:5, God tells us He will never ever leave us or forsake us. As I draw my thoughts to a close, I would like to offer an old hymn that has been around for a while. It was written by Ada Habershon back in 1908. It fell out of favor for a while, but the modern hymn writers Matt Merker and Keith Getty recently rediscovered it and breathed new life into it. I found that as I watched Diane (and then two years later as I watched my mom) succumb to the ravages of cancer, the words of the hymn gave me great comfort.

He Will Hold Me Fast

When I fear my faith will fail,
Christ will hold me fast;
When the tempter would prevail,
He can hold me fast!

> *Refrain:*
> *He will hold me fast,*
> *He will hold me fast;*
> *For my Savior loves me so,*
> *He will hold me fast.*

I could never keep my hold,
He must hold me fast;
For my love is often cold,
He must hold me fast.
I am precious in His sight,
He will hold me fast;
Those He saves are His delight,
He will hold me fast.
He'll not let my soul be lost,
Christ will hold me fast;
Bought by Him at such a cost,
He will hold me fast.

Refrain:
He will hold me fast,
He will hold me fast;
For my Savior loves me so,
He will hold me fast.

—Ada Ruth Habershon (1861-1918)

We live in a broken and battered world, and each of us has made our own individual contributions to this brokenness. But remember: God will never leave or forsake you. In Psalm 139, David tells us that even if we make our bed in Sheol—the Hebrew name for the resting place of the dead—God will be present there with us. In Romans 12, Paul also assures us that not even death can separate us from the love of Christ. Moreover, as 1 John 4:4 tells us, "Greater is He who is in you than he who is in the world." Often it is when things look the darkest that God's light shines the brightest.

I must confess that sometimes I feel like Thomas the doubter. I am overwhelmed by the darkness of this present world. I am encouraged, therefore, by the gentle way in which our Lord dealt with Thomas. You may remember that Jesus appeared to His disciples several times after His resurrection. Thomas, however, was not present on the first occasion, and he refused to believe the reports that Jesus was alive. He said that unless he saw Jesus with his own eyes and put his fingers into Jesus' nail-scarred hands, he could not believe. Jesus then appeared to the disciples again. This time, Thomas was there. So Jesus beckoned him to His side, and with much mercy—without scolding or reprimanding—Jesus held out His hands so Thomas might believe. I am thankful the Lord has also been merciful with me.

Sometimes I find the challenges of this life seem overwhelming, and doubts creep into my soul. I wondered what God was doing when Diane lost her physical battle with cancer. As you can imagine, I had some long conversations with God. I had many questions for Him, and I offered several suggestions as to how He might better run His universe. There were times when I wondered, "God, are you listening? Do you still love me? If so, how much do you love me?" It is in times such as these that Jesus once again makes Himself known. He extends his nail-scarred hands as wide as the cross and says, "I love you this much, and I will never let you go."[1]

1. The following picture is *Cristo Crucificado (Christ Crucified)* by Diego Velázque de Silva (1599-1560) and it is in the permanent collection of the Museo del Prado, Madrid, Spain.

14

Epilogue: The Fingerprint of God

*But the goal of our instruction is love from a pure heart,
from a good conscience, and from a sincere faith.*

—1 Timothy 1:5

*What then shall we say to these things? If God is for us,
who is against us? He who did not spare His own Son,
but delivered Him over for us all, how will He not also
with Him freely give us all things? Who will bring charges
against God's elect? God is the one who justifies; who is
the one who condemns? Christ Jesus is He who died, but
rather, was raised, who is at the right hand of God, who
also intercedes for us. Who will separate us from the love
of Christ? Will tribulation, or trouble, or persecution,
or famine, or nakedness, or danger, or sword? Just as it
is written: "For Your sake we are killed all day long; we
were regarded as sheep to be slaughtered."*

*But in all these things we overwhelmingly conquer
through Him who loved us. For I am convinced that neither
death, nor life, nor angels, nor principalities, nor things
present, nor things to come, nor powers, nor height, nor
depth, nor any other created thing will be able to separate
us from the love of God that is in Christ Jesus our Lord.*

—Romans 8:31-39

Bibliography

St. Augustine. *Homilies on the Gospel of John*, tractate XXVI.13, translated and edited by Philip Schaff in *Nicene and Post-Nicene Fathers, First Series, Volume VII*.

Barna, George. *America at the Crossroads*. Grand Rapids: Baker Books, 2016.

Calvin, John. *Institutes of the Christian Religion*, edited by John T. McNeill and translated by Ford Lewis Battles. Philadelphia: Westminster Press, 1960.

Holt-Lunstad, Julianne, Timothy B. Smith, and J. Bradley Layton. "Social Relationships and Mortality Risk: A Meta-analytic Review." July 27, 2010. https://doi.org/10.1371/journal.pmed.1000316.

Johns Hopkins Medical Center. "Forgiveness: Your Health Depends on It." https://www.hopkinsmedicine.org/health/wellness-and-prevention/forgiveness-your-health-depends-on-it.

Lewis, C. S. *The Screwtape Letters*. HarperCollins: New York, 2001.

Mayo Clinic. "Forgiveness: Letting Go of Grudges and Bitterness." November 4, 2017. *https://www.mayoclinic.org › forgiveness › art-20047692*

Pascal, Blaise. *Pensées*, translated by A.J. Krailsheimer. New York: Penguin Books, 1966, revised edition 1995

Made in the USA
Middletown, DE
30 March 2023

27942761R00070